# Bright Money

## Build Your Personal Wealth And Budgeting Skills

Written by:

**EMIL COLLINS**

# COPYRIGHT

executed to present accurate, up to date, and reliable, complete information. No warranties of any kind are declared or implied. Readers acknowledge that the author is not engaging in the rendering of legal, financial, medical or professional advice. The content within this book has been derived from various sources. Please consult a licensed professional before attempting any techniques outlined in this book.

By reading this document, the reader agrees that under no circumstances is the author responsible for any losses, direct or indirect, which are incurred as a result of the use of the information contained within this document, including, but not limited to, errors, omissions, or inaccuracies.

# TABLE OF CONTENTS

# Just For You!

**A FREE GIFT TO OUR READERS**

Ready-to-use templates that you can download and start mind mapping with right away!

**Visit this Link**

https://infobusiness001us.activehosted.com/f/1

# PREFACE

> **Do you want to set up a budget and start saving money smartly to fulfil your dreams and support your family at the same time? Then look no further as this is the book for you!**

No matter what people say, the truth is money indeed is the single most essential element that makes the world go round. No matter what you want to do, it will cost you money.

We all know that saving money is hard, and it is even harder if you live on a paycheck-to-paycheck basis. But does it always have to be that way? Not really! No matter where you are from or your income level, it is possible to save some money and lead a healthy and normal life. What you need are some smart budgeting skills and the know-how to implement them.

This book titled **"Bright Money: Build Your Personal Wealth And Budgeting Skills"** has been written from the ground up to help you do just that and more. With the skills, strategies and information share within this book, you will be able to set up the perfect budget plan for you, based on your income/expenditure level and build up savings that will not only keep your family safe but also allow you to fulfil some of the dreams that you've been bottling up!

The core ideas that you will discover in this book include;

- Understand more about the concept of budgeting and where it originated more. Know about the importance of budgeting and why do you even need it!
- Know how you can set smart budgeting goals and understand the importance of
- Learn to analyze your income and your expenses to make smart decisions.
- Get the steps of what you should do if your expenditure exceeds your budget and know more about strategies such as Bare Bone Budgeting.
- Know about the different strategies through which you can save money, including the 50-

30-20 System, Envelope System and the Zero-Based Budget System

- Understand the different tools, that you can use to keep track of your budget, starting from simple worksheets to robust computer and mobile programs.
- Understand the importance of tracking your budget and learn the process of evaluating and reviewing it.
- Learn excellent strategies to help you stick to your budget and make the process of budgeting fun.
- Know how to smartly invest your money in the short term and long term savings for a better tomorrow.

And a lot more!

This is essentially a goldmine of information for those looking to take their first step towards creating the perfect budget!

> **So, If you want to discover how to create the perfect budget plan by analyzing your income/expenditure and follow it through to a better tomorrow, then buy this book right now! This is the stepping**

**stone that will guide you towards building a more defined financial structure for you and your family.**

# INTRODUCTION

Some people might argue that America is in a really good shape, and the citizens have all of their financial needs figured out from the outside. Unfortunately, that's far away from the truth. While the rise of the pandemic has inspired more and more people to start saving and budgeting, the majority of the population is sadly still living on a paycheck-to-paycheck basis!

Let me share some statistics to paint the whole picture. Willis Tower Watson claimed that almost 18% of workers who had a salary of more than $100,000 still live on a paycheck-to-paycheck basis. Not only that, 59% of all U.S adults are still living paycheck to paycheck, according to Schwab! Another 28% confessed that they had absolutely no savings/emergency funding of their own!

That's just going through the surface. The deeper you go, the darker it gets. Since you are reading this book, I would assume that you are one of those static, and even if you were not interested in it before, I am pretty sure that the Pandemic has inspired you to start planning your very own budget.

I don't blame you; the Pandemic has been hard on everybody. Companies, factories are getting shut, and people are losing their jobs left and right. This is a type of crisis that we never expected to face in this modern world; a mere virus brings the whole world down to its knees.

Even before the pandemic hit, there was once a time when I, too, had to live on a very tight and suffocating budget. Everything felt very suffocating, and the restrictions literally made it impossible to do anything that I wanted. But eventually, I started to practice budgeting, I encouraged my family to start saving money. I got rid of all my debts and created emergency funding for the future.

It took us a bit of time to pull through; with the help of my family and some smart decisions, we were able to pass through the difficult times and now have good savings under our belt with a secured future planned out. I mean, we can never be 100% prepared for what's to come, but at least now, we are not living on a paycheck basis!

This is something I had to understand the hard way, but you don't have to. When I reached absolute financial rock bottom, I resolved to strictly regulate my financial efforts. My family was completely behind me, so I began studying different methods of saving money and how a person can use the money saved to invest in a sound business plan. It took some time for me to get things right. Nonetheless, thanks to our growing passion for saving money together and my internal desire to start a company, I was able to save enough money to completely support my family and our life and launch a profitable Kindle Publication that has been supporting us ever. Since!

It took me a while, and it wasn't easy, but my perseverance and hard work paid off in the end.

And it all began with a desire to save money. One of the most critical aspects of accumulating resources and having a secure financial future is saving money. Saving money helps you to avoid the uncertainties of life and enjoy a more satisfying life. Putting money aside in a systematic manner would help you escape many pitfalls and obstacles in life. It will be of assistance to you in your hour of need and will ensure that your family has something to fall back on in the event of a tragedy.

But here's the thing, some people get really afraid of budgeting, thinking that they would have to sacrifice everything they love to save a dime. The truth isn't like that!

The fact is that budgeting does not imply sacrifice; rather, it implies freedom of choice. A budget is a financial plan that allows you to take charge of your finances and have all of the things you want, whatever they are.

You can tailor your budget to your desired lifestyle, whether it is absolute financial security, the freedom to quit your job and travel the world, or the money to buy your dream home and start a family.

Budgeting is the process of creating a plan for financial stability and growth. Sometimes that means cutting back on expenses (especially those that aren't providing you with any benefits);

other times, making room for big life changes: (like buying a house). It is a method of wisely using your resources and transforming them into potential capital.

Other than that, it's a way to take the stress out of money management: instead of worrying about any bill that comes in, for example, you'll already know how to pay it. You'll have a plan in place to get rid of the debt that's been keeping you up at night. You won't have to be concerned with having enough money to support your retirement. That financial trust will assist you in overcoming the obstacles that have been preventing you from progressing and accumulating a healthy nest egg.

To get to your desired financial destination, you must first understand where you are starting from. You'll use the knowledge to chart a path that will help you achieve your objectives. Your budget will serve as your GPS, directing you and rerouting you when detours arise, allowing you to get to your destination.

So, whether you are already an individual who is going through a difficult financial phase or are someone who wants to prepare themselves for their next emergency, this book is for you!

The book has been written in a very simple and easy-to-follow manner so that anyone can effortlessly pick it up and start grasping the concepts.

Following the concepts that are shared in this book, you will be able to:

- Get total peace of mind knowing that you have enough budget saved for an emergency fund to support your family for days to come
- Have enough money set aside to fulfill your desires and dreams and not just finish every single penny on wants
- Be able to control your expenditure and save more on the side
- Be able to smartly invest in both long term and short goal to acquire a secure future

Most importantly,

- Be able to create a full-proof and well-designed plan that would protect you and your family from a sudden financial crisis if any major expense arrives.

The bottom line is that if you are looking for anything relating to budgeting and how to start your budget, this book right here has you covered.

Those of you who want an idea of the topics covered here, let me give you a general idea.

- Understand the importance of budgeting, the origin of budgeting, and know why is it such a crucial part of your financial wellbeing.
- Learn how to define your financial goals in a SMART way. Here, we have shared several different tactics and strategies that you can follow to set yourself on the right path.
- Know how to analyze your monthly income and expenses properly.
- Understand how to develop your budget plan and how you can start saving more money to grow your budget.
- Know about the different tools that you can use to track your budget.
- Understand how you can stick to your designed budget plan by not making it boring
- Know how you can smartly invest your saved money in long-term and short-term prospects and get the most benefit out of them!

And much more!

Now, that we are done with the intro, let's slide into the first chapter of this book, where I start by walking you through the origin of the concept of budgeting and where it came from!

# CHAPTER ONE

# The Importance Of Budgeting And Its Effect On Our Finances

Before going into the deeper concepts, I believe that it is essential that you know what Budgeting really is and why it is so important.

## The Origin Of The Budgeting Concept

As a planning and control tool, the theoretical and practical foundations of the Budget had their origin in the government sector at the end of the 18th century.

when the spending plans of the kingdom were presented to the British Parliament, and guidelines were given on their possible execution and control.

This meaning was later refined in the English system with the term common knowledge budget, which in our language is called Budget. In 1820, France introduced the scheme in the government sector. In 1821, the United States welcomed it as a component of public expenditure regulation and as a foundation for the need articulated by officials tasked with budgeting to ensure the efficient operation of government activities.

Between 1912 and 1925, and especially after the First World War, the private sector realized the benefits that the Budget could generate in terms of cost control and allocated resources in those aspects necessary to obtain adequate profit margins during a period—determined operating cycle. In this period, industries multiply, and the use of appropriate business planning methods is considered. There is intense talk of budgetary control in private companies, and in the public sector, a National Budget Law is even passed.

The methodology continued to evolve in tandem with the advancements made by cost accounting.

Consider the Westinghouse Company, which introduced the standard cost system in 1928 after agreeing to the treatment in the variation of the specific operation volumes of the "flexible budget" system. This innovation supports the need for budgeting and preparation and technicality, group work, and decision-making based on systematic cost research and evaluation.

The basic principles of the framework were described at the First International Symposium on Budgetary Control in Geneva in 1930. The United States Department of Navy proposed the Budget for Programs and Operations in 1948.

In 1961, the United States Department of Defense used a program-and-budget preparation scheme. In 1965, the United States government established the Budget Department, which became part of the system's planning and control tools known as "planning by programs and budgets."

The importance of budgets is emphasized by prestigious contemporary authors, who emphasize the importance of cash management forecasts. A process of development and modernization of the Budget was carried out, in which two new classifications were adopted, the annual publication of a document on Budget Execution was initiated, and more complete instructions for the presentation of preliminary draft budgets by programs, structuring the chapters in programs, subprograms, and activities, at all levels of the Budget, were incorporated. This process culminated on December 11, 1969, with the passage of Law No. 531, or the "Organic Budget Law for the Public Sector," which remained in force until December 31, 2006. This was the most important legislative tool in the Dominican Republic for budget control. It widened the budget's reach.

In the Dominican Republic, the financial administration reform process started in 1996. With the establishment of the Integrated Financial Management Program (PAFI) and the IDB's technical-financial assistance (a loan of US $ 12.0 mm), the implementation of the Integrated Financial Management System (SIGEF) was made possible, which connects the System's governing bodies i.e. ONAPRES, the Directorate of Government Accounting (DIGECOG), Public

Credit (DCP), National Treasury (TN) and online (Internal Control, GCR).

The legislative framework for the country's financial administration reform process was completed in January 2007 to achieve greater accountability and rationality in using State resources. In this regard, administrative laws were enacted, one of which established the Secretary of State for Finance (previously Finance) as the governing body of the State Financial Administration, in charge of fiscal policy, the financial system, and the multiyear Budget—centralizing budgetary functions such as budgeting, collection operations, and other revenue, expenditures, and financing.

The Organic Budget Law for the Public Sector No. 42306 of November 17, 2006, renamed ONAPRES as the General Budget Directorate (DIGEPRES), and established it as the Governing Body of the Budgetary System, with this new designation, making it a dependency of the Secretary of State for Finance, rather than the previous link with the Technical Secretariat of the Presidium.

As an integral part of the reform process, this event represented a new and modern budget regime.

## What Does Budgeting Stand For?

A budget is a document that converts plans into dollars - dollars that will need to be spent to complete the planned activities (expenditure) and dollars that will need to be produced to cover the price of completing the work (generation) (income). An estimation, or educated guess, of how much money you'll need to achieve your mission.

Many people consider budgeting to be something they can do only when they are low on cash. Students can use a budget to figure out how to make ends meet in light of their high expenses and limited incomes. New graduates who are financially savvy create budgets to ensure that their first paychecks are adequately split between emergency savings, retirement savings, student loan repayments, and other expenditures. Budgets are often made by young couples trying to figure out how to afford a wedding or newlyweds trying to figure out how to incorporate the cost of buying a house or raising a child into their monthly cash flow. Budgets are, of course, widely associated with people of all ages who are struggling to make ends meet. The fact is that budgeting isn't just about when your finances are tight or your life is going through a major change. All, rich or poor, have to budget. If your budget regularly, it will be much easier to access during times of transition. Without proper budgeting, where do you think a Fortune 500 business like Amazon will be today? What about the wealthy?

In the business context, we usually mean the Budget, which is the document in which all the revenue and expenditure forecasts refer to a period of exercise or an entire year are reported. In addition to the company's whole business, it can also refer to a specific sector (for example, a company division) or a single action (for example, an advertising campaign).

## Why Do You Need A Budget?

1. **It assists you in keeping your focus on the target:**

A budget will assist you in determining and achieving your long-term objectives. How would you ever save enough money to buy a car, go on that holiday, or put a down payment on a house if you wander through life, tossing your money at any beautiful, shiny thing that happens to catch your eye? It means that you do not waste money you do not have: We owe it all to credit cards, where much too many customers waste money they don't have. In 2020, the total credit card debt per household will be $7,027.

People used to tell whether they were living beyond their means before the advent of plastic. They were on target if they had enough money left over at the end of the month to pay their bills and set some money back in savings. People who overspend and misuse credit cards these days don't always know they're doing so until they're in debt.

You can never find yourself in this precarious situation if you build and stick to a budget. You'll know exactly how much money

- You make.
- You can spend each month.

- You must put aside.

Keep in mind that by the time your spendthrift mates make an appointment for debt counseling next year, you'll be on the way to the European vacation you've been saving for—or, better yet, move to a new home.

2. **It Leads to a More Comfortable Retirement:**

Let's say you never have credit card debt because you use your money wisely, stick to your budget diligently, and never overspend. That's awesome! But don't you think there's something you're overlooking? As important as it is to invest your money wisely now, it is also vital to prepare for the future.

A budget will assist you in accomplishing this. It's essential to factor investment contributions into your financial plan. You can build a nice nest egg if you set aside a portion of your earnings per month to contribute to your IRA, 401(k), or other retirement funds. While you might have to make some sacrifices now, it will be well worth it in the long run.

3. **It Helps You Prepare for Emergencies:**

It Assists You in Preparing for Emergencies. In life, of which some are better than others. When you lose your job, become ill or disabled, divorce, or have a family member die, you can find yourself in serious financial issues. Of course, these crises always seem to strike at the worst possible time—when you're already short on cash. This is the reason everybody should have an emergency fund. An emergency fund with at least three to six months' worth of living expenses should be included in your budget. This extra cash will save you from spiraling into debt as a result of a life crisis. Of course, saving three to six months' worth of expenses would take time.

Do not automatically invest the rest of your paycheck into your emergency fund. Create a budget for it, set reasonable targets, and start tiny. Even if you just set aside $10 to $3o a week, your emergency fund would expand over time.

4. **It Helps in the Exposure of Poor Spending Habits:**

You are forced to examine your spending patterns when creating a budget. You may find that you're wasting money on items that you don't need. Do you still watch all 500 channels on your outrageous cable package? Do you need so many pairs of black shoes? Budgeting enables you to reconsider your expenditure patterns and refocus your financial objectives.

5. **It's Better Than Sheep Counting:**

Maintaining a budget would also assist you in getting more sleep. How many times have you tossed and turned trying to figure out how you're going to pay your bills? People who cannot sleep at night due to financial difficulties are allowing their money to control them. Take command of the situation once more. If you budget carefully, you'll never have to think about finances again. There are many other benefits of sticking to a budget. So, what do you have to lose? It's time to get serious about budgeting!

A budget forces you to plan out your objectives, save money, monitor your success, and turn your ambitions into reality. Okay, so it hurts when you know you can't afford the brand-new Xbox game or the beautiful cashmere sweater in the shop window. It would be much easier to turn around and walk out of the shop empty-handed if you remind yourself that you're saving for a new home

## Why Is Having A Budget Important

- Budgets help an organization to build a financial roadmap by defining targets and working toward them.
- A budget will assist an organization in assessing goals and, as a result, better managing spending, resulting in increased revenues.
- A budget would allow a company to be more prepared for significant capital projects and help recognize potential investment opportunities.
- Budget make us understand the set of expenses and inputs that a person, entity, or government can foresee for a given period concerning its finances, the uses and objectives assigned to each item or expense, and the uses and long-term forecasts of available funds.
- The idea of a budget always supposes a forecast of personal or state finances. To make a budget, some anticipation is required not only of the expenses that must be made in the determined time but also of the profits or capital inflows that it may mean that period.

In some cases, the Budget is an item that can be set individually (for example, when a person analyzes their Budget).

In other cases, the Budget involves an agreement between the parties if there is more than one (for example, when two or more people decide what to spend or whether a government will use available resources in such a way).

## It Acts As A Foresight

The Budget, as the name suggests, is a presumption in finance and economics about the operations or movements to be carried out in a future timeframe that is estimated roughly. When we talk about the government or state budget, we usually mean budgets that are prepared to account for a plethora of variables related to the various economic activities in the region, such as work projects or new government measures, possible debt payments or international fees, extra expenses, and even the forecast of possible alterations to the original Budget based on the results of the research. The government budget has a unique feature: in most nations, it must be decided upon by the Executive Power and the

Legislative Power, including members from different parties and political expressions. This is to avoid the presidents' or those in executive roles' discretion in deciding on current funds and services in isolation. It is assumed that if those in administrative and legislative roles do not belong to the same party, the Budget would not be accepted, posing a barrier to governance.

Other subjects' budgets, such as individuals' or particular agencies', may also be reduced to periods longer or shorter than a year. For example, a work schedule that lasts longer than a year but takes less than a year is planned.

The core of the Budget is a need to order finances to include both short-term and long-term projections.

A budget will help you prepare for short-term costs like monthly payments, mid-term costs like holidays, and long-term costs like buying a home, planning for a child's college education, and saving for retirement. You'll always know when you need to cut back on spending when you can afford to loosen the lines, and how long it will take to save for big goals if you have a spreadsheet or notebook in front of you that shows how much money you expect to make for the next few months (or years), how much of that money goes out every month, and how much money you have left to save each month. If you're unhappy with your numbers, knowing what they are will help you take steps to improve your situation, whether it's focusing on paying off credit cards to increase your monthly cash flow, having a promotion, or switching jobs to save enough money to purchase anything you need and want.

The significance of this Budget is always in making a thorough and well-founded forecast of the global, monetary, and financial movements that will define the subject who performs it. Thus, without the Budget, instability can easily be created by incurring more expenditures than necessary or failing to manage revenues or capital inflows.

According to experts, getting a clear idea of the individual or family Budget will benefit us tremendously in finances, helping us know which tasks are guaranteed priority and relegated to the background. They also establish that as individuals or families become more humble, the budget allotted to food and necessities increases to 80%. In contrast, in households with more buying power, this may also fall to 50%, so there is more opportunity to use the remaining budget for other things and needs such as entertainment, better healthcare, schooling, etc. This is, in other words, what forecasting means since alternatives to using the money or even favoring saving can be preferred in situations where it is not available due to commodity prices, inflation, and so on.

As can be seen, the financial Budget makes the funds available to be more precisely arranged according to needs, even encouraging long-term forecasting and potential expenditure, or saving of a couple's, families, or institution's economic activities.

A business that does not have a budget runs the risk of being caught off guard. Suppose a corporation does not set aside funds for unexpected expenses and acquisitions.

In that case, it runs the risk of failing to meet its obligations when they are due. Without a budget, the organization risks having expenses consume its revenue, reducing earnings and ultimately jeopardizing its survival.

## Advantages Of Setting A Budget

A budget has many fundamental advantages. The most important ones are listed below:

**1. Keeps you organized.**

A budget will help you keep your finances sorted because it entails a structured, logical, and formal approach to record your financials, thus enabling robust money management. It provides clarity and transparency over your cash flows of the past, the present, and the (foreseeable) future.

**2. Keeps you in control.**

Maybe you heard the saying "Being in control of your money means being in control of your life" by **Manages debts.** If you have no debts but decided to take out a loan, a budget shows you how much debt repayment you could sensibly shoulder. If you have debts, a budget aids you to focus and incentivizes you to pay off debts quickly so that you can unchain your money and use it for more value-adding purposes (such as for savings, for example).

**3. Builds wealth.**

A budget ensures that you have enough money to prepare for emergencies, retirement, and the accomplishment of your goals. Such savings are required as a prerequisite for investments that are required to achieve your long-term financial goals. You will create healthy spending levels, reduce debts, allow reasonable saving rates, and ensure future investments if you practice continuous budget discipline. As your net worth grows over time, you will invariably be accumulating money. The difference between what you own and what you owe is net worth: total assets minus total liabilities.

Now, that we've discussed the advantages of using a budget, you might be wondering if there are any drawbacks. That's an excellent topic. Budget opponents have the following to say:

Sam Beckbessinger full name is Samuel Beckbessinger. A budget puts you in control. It allows you to regain power and prevents you from becoming a slave to your finances. Before you even receive or touch your money, you know where it is going (or isn't going) and how you are supposed (or aren't supposed) to spend it. A budget prevents the money from dragging you down. Instead, you are the one who consciously and purposefully guides your funds.

4. **Induces discipline and prevents overspending.**

A budget induces self-restraint and pre-determines your spending decisions in advance. It ensures your money is spent responsibly. That way, you are much more likely to live within permissible monetary limits by spending less than you earn and saving more.

5. **Enables the achievement of your goals.**

A budget provides a framework guiding your decisions and financial habits. Through proper planning, you ensure that your financial routines, such as saving and spending, are conducted in a way that you can reach your desired objectives.

6. **Signals a call to action.**

Budgeting alerts us to whether we need to earn more, spend less, or save more to stay financially afloat and achieve our financial goals. It identifies gaps between different categories of cash inflows and outflows, warning us if we need to correct course. Therefore, you are more likely to foresee and cope with financial bottlenecks that may lie ahead of you through budgeting.

**7. Enables communication.**

You will be surprised to know that many spouses do not discuss finances because they feel insecure talking about sensitive, albeit crucial, topics. True, money has the power to stir up emotions, and it is indeed often a topic to fight about. However, a budget can also be used as a "tranquilizer," as it facilitates and permits you to communicate calmly, factually, and effectively.

**8. Manages debts.**

If you have no debts but decided to take out a loan, a budget shows you how much debt repayment you could sensibly shoulder. If you have debts, a budget aids you to focus and incentivizes you to pay off debts quickly so that you can unchain your money and use it for more value-adding purposes (such as for savings).

9. **Builds wealth.**

   A budget helps you to ensure you have sufficient funds to save for emergencies, retirement, and the achievement of your goals. Such savings are a prerequisite for investments that are mandatory to accomplish your long-term financial goals. By applying continuous budget discipline, you will establish healthy spending levels, reduce debts, enable decent saving rates, and ensure subsequent investments. Inevitably, you will therefore be building wealth as your net worth increases over time. Net worth is defined as the difference between what you own and what you owe: total assets minus total liabilities.

## Drawbacks Of Budgeting To Keep In Mind

Now, that we have looked at the benefits of using a budget, you might be asking if there are any disadvantages too? Good question. Here is what the critics say about budgets:

Sam Beckbessinger. A budget puts you in command. It helps you take control and avoids you being a slave to your finances. Before you even receive or touch your money, you know where it's destined (not) to go and how you are supposed (not) to spend it. A budget prohibits your money from pushing you around. Instead, you are the one who pro-actively directs your funds with purposefulness.

### 1. Bureaucratic.

Admittedly, a budget requires a certain degree of formality. While, I am a fan of keeping things simple, I do not see how one could do a budget completely without any formal means. But, I agree that we should not overdo it. And as you will see, luckily, there are quite a few formidable ways to make our budgeting lives much more convenient.

### 2. Inaccurate

Budgeting can be difficult if you have not been able to keep good records or reliable financial details. Start keeping meticulous records of your profits and expenditures if you haven't already. Tax returns, pay stubs, receipts, bills, bank statements, and other documents fall under this category.

When creating a budget, these documents will eliminate inaccuracies. However, even though you have all of the requisite records at your fingertips, you can still experience inaccuracies due to recording or forecasting errors. However, I am convinced that a slightly off-budget is much superior to getting no budget at all.

### 3. Time-consuming.

Budgeting may seem time-consuming, especially in the beginning. However, we will touch on several hacks and digital tools that can streamline the entire process. In the end, and while it may still be inconvenient to take an estimated hour each month to analyze your personal budget, it is time well spent.

### 4. Rigid.

Budgeting may force strict limits on your spending habits that you might sometimes perceive as unfair. For example, you might not be able to go on this cherished shopping spree because of budget restrictions imposed by yourself. But guess what, it's okay to say no. Such discipline is necessary and unavoidable to ensure you save and invest required funds, thus increasing your wealth over time **Kills the fun factor**. Budgeting does not imply sacrificing the enjoyable aspects of your existence. Anything, including entertainment, is manageable if you prepare ahead of time. The only way budgeting will destroy the fun element is if you allow your money to dominate your life rather than handling it efficiently and intelligently.

To summarize, we must recognize that budgeting requires commitment. Financial preparation can be time-consuming.

However, nothing comes from nothing, as we all know. If you want to be in charge of your finances and continually develop them, you must use a budget to guide and track your spending. What we should discuss (and optimize) is the level of preparation and formalism to be used. More on this in subsequent chapters.

**5. A little forethought goes a long way.**

A personal budget will help you remain structured and in charge of your finances. It improves contact and allows for financial management. A budget gives you visibility, transparency, and early notice, keeping you from making poor financial decisions. It instills discipline in spending less, paying off loans, saving more, and investing. As a result, a budget helps you build your net worth over time and is your best chance of meeting your financial objectives. Despite the extra work required, a budget is essential for establishing and defending your financial well-being.

# CHAPTER TWO

# Setting A Goal And Starting With Your Budgeting Process

Now that you have a good idea about Budgeting, let's walk you through setting up your personal goal.

## Importance Of Setting Up A Budget Goal

Building wealth is easy, but it does take some time and effort. As in any activity, whether it's growing a business or learning a new skill, you should establish your long-term objectives early on. It's the same when it comes to accumulating wealth; it's important to set financial goals.

Setting financial goals is important for making financial progress. Once you've established your goals, you will devise and carry out a strategy to achieve them.

It helps you stay focused and ensures you're on the right track. Without further ado, here are seven reasons why you should set financial goals and how they will help you achieve them.

### 1. Know Where You Are Going

What are you trying to achieve? What does success entail for you?

Setting financial goals will help you answer both of these questions. You will know your ultimate goal and what you need to do to get there if you have your answers, which will be exclusive to you and your personal and professional circumstances.

We also can make meaningful changes in our lives, with the ultimate goal of making the right decisions easier.

### 2. Helps You Understand How Much Money You Can Save

How much money do you need to invest and save to achieve your financial objectives?

Setting financial goals helps you to measure and quantify your plans.

If your target is £5,000, £1,500,000, or higher, you can monitor your progress and change your strategy if you want to speed things up. It makes financial planning much easier.

If you're having difficulty saving money? You will start saving money automatically by using money-saving apps like Plum. The app is a fantastic way to start saving money without missing out. Setting financial goals helps you to measure and quantify your plans.

3. **Different Goals Will Ask You To Employ Different Strategies**

Your financial objectives will determine the tactics you will need to use to achieve them. If your financial targets are moderate, it might be sufficient to save a little extra per month.

Suppose you have larger goals, such as buying a home, retiring early, or taking a year off to travel. In that case, you will need to combine various strategies to raise your income, reduce expenses, and invest your savings in stocks or bonds to expand your money faster.

Once you've determined your financial objectives, you will determine which methods are best for you.

### 4. They Will Influence Your Career Choices

Setting financial goals can influence your decision-making in your career.

If your ambitions are ambitious, you will need to consider how much time you can afford to take off, what you need to do to get a promotion or a pay raise, and so on.

Realizing certain financial goals can necessitate leaving the stability of a 9 to 5 job and starting your own company, which, while risky, can be more lucrative in the long run. Your career preparation and financial planning will complement each other when you know what your financial goals are.

### 5. Financial Goals Will Keep You Focused

Another significant factor why it is important to set financial targets is that it assists you in staying focused. Setting financial targets will assist you in keeping your eyes on the prize. It's well worth taking a snapshot of one or more of your ambitions — whether it's a home, a car, or work you can do from the beach — and pinning it to the wall next to your desk.

This will help you stick to your guns when you're tempted to splurge on something you don't need, as well as remind you of why you're putting in extra hours. In this scenario, the result justifies the means, which will keep you on track.

### 6. Help You Find The Right Tools To Assist

There are thousands of resources available to help you save, raise more money, and invest your money. Many of these are free to download from the App Store or Google Play, but some require a subscription or a charge to download. For example, you can use the **Wealthily** app to start saving with as little as £1, save automatically with Plum, or monitor your money with Cleo.

Setting financial targets will allow you to objectively assess which resources to support you along the way, allowing you to purchase only those that will be most useful to you. It is pointless to waste money on unnecessary items; instead, save your money on what will benefit you the most.

## 7. Will Give You A Sense Of Accomplishment

Realizing your financial goals can be a lengthy and time-consuming task. On the other hand, setting financial targets is the first step, and it requires both thought and discipline. Writing them down is an accomplishment in and of itself, so you're justified in congratulating yourself after you've completed it.

Give yourself a pat on the back for embarking on your new financial adventure and having already overcome the first hurdle. Setting financial objectives is the first step toward achieving them. Setting financial objectives is the first step toward achieving them. You don't have to go it alone; in truth, those who seek assistance are much more likely to succeed.

Before you develop your budget, you must reflect on your "why." In other words, you need to know why you need a budget and what it should serve you for.

While you might have many aims and expectations, on a high level, you want your budget to deliver the following two main services:

- Help you operationalize your action plan to achieve your financial goals; and
- Help you to become and remain financially healthy.

## Things You Want Your Budget To Cover

Typically, everything else that you want your budget to do for you falls within one of these two points listed above.

**1. Financial goals**

As you might recall from my second book in the "Money Mind Series," financial goals include a path for a life full of purpose, concentration, inspiration, and achievement. Ideation strategies (such as brainstorming or reverse thinking) can help you create an initial list of possible goals and inspire innovation.

To stop changing your goals as often as your socks, you should fine-tune this list and select goals that are truly long-term. SMART (Specific, Measurable, Attainable, Relevant, Time-bound) goals must be SMART (Specific, Measurable, Attainable, Relevant, Time-bound), true (genuinely your own), under your direct control (can be influenced), "just right" (not too hard and not too easy), and inspire your passion.

You can refine your goals and prioritize them based on price, importance, time, and implementation effort. If you've settled on your final list of financial objectives, create a course of action to make them a reality. An action plan deconstructs larger goals into smaller, more manageable, less daunting, and easier to implement. Then, once your objectives are met, begin executing your action plan and bask in the invincible feeling of pride and accomplishment.

Your financial objectives and action plan will put to good use. Rest assured that our budgeting exercise will greatly increase your chances of meeting your goals and enjoying a financially stress-free life.

## 2. Financial health

Ok, now the going gets tough. We need to get our hands dirty. But don't be scared that this could be complicated because it really isn't. Having said this, when you are going through the budgeting exercise for the first time, it might surely feel a bit unfamiliar and odd. Be brave and stand tall. You need to get through this once. Over time, it will become a routine that you will actually enjoy doing. You will see.

Every recipe has several ingredients. The same holds true for your budget. If you want your budget to show you the way and indicate your financial health, you need to first feed "the beast" with data. Financial data that is.

Here is the financial information we need to capture for your monthly budget:

**Income** You need to collect all sources of your current earnings (net, after taxes)

**Savings rate** You need to determine how much to save to cover for unexpected emergencies, to prepare for retirement, and to achieve your financial goals (we will further elaborate on this in a moment)

3. **Expenses**
   - Past receipts for all of your monthly expenses, such as rent, food, housing, clothing, travel, internet, phone bills, maintenance, entertainment, insurance, utilities, club memberships, and so on, must be collected.
   - You must be aware of the monthly payments for mortgages, loans, credit card debt, auto payments, and so on.
   - The same is true with any tax payments (based on past tax declarations etc.)

To avoid confusion, let me preface how we will be dealing with your budget as of the next chapter, so you understand why this first, although boring, phase is important. The budget formula we'll use as a foundation for subsequent review is as follows:

**Income - Savings - Expenses = Financial Health.** There will be more on this later.

Following that, we'll look at some additional notes to keep in mind while preparing your budget.

## 4. Monthly budget

You can prepare a budget for any period you deem appropriate and meaningful. However, a monthly budget is a norm (whereas an annual budget is a standard). So, while we are focusing on a monthly budget, you can apply the same approach for any other period you desire.

## 5. Single versus multi-user budget

Before you start, decide if the budget is for you alone, for you and your partner, or the entire family (should you have one). If the budget is for you and your partner, go through the exercise jointly.

Remember that income, expense, and saving amounts have to be reflective of all parties involved. In other words, you need to collect receipts and capture relevant financial amounts for yourself and all other participants in the same budget.

## 6. Monthly versus non-monthly income and expenses

When recording your income and expenses, make sure to provide all details relevant to a particular month. Calculate averages for non-monthly revenue and expenditures to include in your monthly budget. Here's an example of earnings:

- If you receive a weekly salary, multiply your earnings by 52. (the number of weeks in a year). Divide the result by 12 (the number of months in a year) to calculate your monthly salary.
- If you collect a bi-weekly salary, multiply your earnings by 26. (the number of paychecks you receive in a year). Divide the result by 12 (the number of months in a year) to calculate your monthly salary.
- If you have an erratic income: If your salary varies over time (for example, because of bonus payments or restaurant tips), you can still work with averages. In this situation, add up multiple months of income and divide by the same number of months you used to total your income previously. For example, if you used four months of

irregular income totaling $1,000, your monthly average would be $250 ($1,000/4 months). In your budget, use this average as your approximate monthly revenue.

Remember to include non-monthly expenditures, for which you can compute averages using the same logic as mentioned above for profits.

For example, you might have quarterly expenses like club memberships or annual expenses like insurance premiums. Be sure not to forget these costs and to prepare for them as well.

### 7. One-off earnings

When I do my budget, I typically plan for all expenses without exceptions. However, I usually do not account for irregular/ad-hoc/one-off income such as tax refunds or potential bonus payments when it comes to my income sources.

I want to keep such income as a positive surprise without pre-allocating it to any specific purpose. Should the income indeed materialize, I welcome these flexible funds, which can be used as an additional financial buffer, for example.

## 8. Savings rate

Savings are critical on your path to financial independence. As mentioned, you need to save for emergencies, retirement, and your financial goals

## 9. Emergencies.

You want to cover at least 3, ideally 6 months' worth of your monthly expenses. When you are starting, consider using 3 months. Once you have reached this intermediate goal, you can be more aggressive and save more.

In any case, as you grow older and your income rises, you should beef up your emergency fund to cover 6 months' worth of your monthly expenses. You should establish your emergency fund within a year.

An example: let's say your monthly expenses amount to $1,000. You decided to initially save 3 months' worth of your monthly expenses as an emergency buffer, which equals $3,000 ($1,000"3 months).

If you want to populate your emergency fund within a year, you must save $250 each month ($3,000/12 months).

**10. Retirement.**

You should save at least 10% of your net income (read: take-home income, after taxes). If you earn $2,000 net each month, at least $200 should go into your long-term savings ($2,000 10%).

**11. Financial goals.**

The savings rate is distinct to each individual. It is determined by what you are striving to achieve. You have previously established your financial goals, priced them out, broken them down, and put them on a timeline. You need to work with this data and convert it into a savings number to be put into your budget.

For example, let's say you decided to buy a house in 5 years and want to save for a required down payment of $18,000. In this case, you need to save $300 every month ($18,000/5 years/12 months). You need to proceed with the same calculations for each one of your financial goals. Every financial goal requires its monthly saving rate.

A piece of advice: you will unlikely have sufficient earnings to save for the entirety of your financial goals at once. Instead, you need to make choices and decide how to sequence your financial goals (when to start saving for which goal).

## 12. Actual versus target amounts

For each income, saving, and expense item in your budget, you need to write down what you earn/save/spend today (retrospective view based on actual) and what you wish to earn/save/spend tomorrow (prospective view based on budget targets). This gives your budget a dear direction because you are literally "telling your money where to go." To put it differently, you give every single dollar its own meaning or destination.

When reviewing your budget, you compare actual with intended, or budgeted, amounts and observe where you are better or worse off. You then know exactly if and where your financial habits need to be modified going forward. This provides a crisp line of sight instructing you where to place your focus on.

Once you are done with all of the above, you need to add up the totals for each of your three main budget ingredients: total income, total savings, total expenses. That's it. You are done with your first budget. Great job! Before we start using your budget to your benefit, we should speak about a few tools which can make your budget preparations more pleasant.

**13. Convenience and accessibility**

We need to make sure budgeting isn't too difficult for you. Fortunately, there are a few resources available that can help. Tell me which side your heart is on: the "ancient physical" approach or the "new digital" gadgets?

You may use paper and pencil to record your feedback on a printed ledger if you prefer it "old-school," which might be fair, particularly when you start budgeting. It's not the most cutting-edge tool, but it works.

The most simple (and still widely used) method for creating a budget and monitoring expenditures is using an electronic spreadsheet (like Excel) if you're into technology. There are several pre-made electronic models available for download (free and paid). They will do the calculations for you once they are set up. If that's your choice, make sure to download a file with a column and line layout that can be modified. This will enable you to incorporate some specific nuances to accurately represent your own financial situation.

Using an app is a more sophisticated interactive solution. Yes, I know that's what you've (most likely) been waiting for. Another excuse to keep fiddling with your phone at all hours of the day and night. It's just that this time it's not mindless gaming but serious business.

There are numerous (free and paid) budgeting applications available to assist you in creating, tracking, and managing your budget. Any of these apps can be connected directly to your bank account. This method automatically logs, categorizes and displays your spending in a beautiful online budget. Amazing technology.

But keep in mind that for this method to function flawlessly, you should preferably pay all of your expenses with the same credit/debit card linked to a single bank account. Otherwise, you'll have a mixture of automated and manual postings of your revenue and spending transactions.

You must experiment with various methods to determine which ones work better for you. However, regardless of the approach you use, whether offline or online, keep it easy and avoid being distracted by the fancy tool you use. A budget is about your ability to maintain the habit of closely watching your financials. If you overcomplicate it or lose concentration, you can become frustrated and abandon budgeting before it begins to produce its true value.

Likely, your first budget would not work for you as expected for various reasons. Don't be discouraged, and don't give up easily. Remember that, like anything else in life, there will be a learning curve. Try again to see for yourself that the budget works even better the second time around. Small steps.

You will find a few selected apps and spreadsheets to try out in the "Resources" chapter at the end of this book. Please remember to change the spreadsheets to represent your specific circumstance and personal preferences.

A budget is a mechanism that allows you to provide a service to yourself. It assists you in meeting your objectives and indicating the state of your finances. A monthly budget is commonly used in the sense of personal finance. All irregular, non-monthly earnings, investments, and expenditures must be (re-)calculated using averages to fit into a monthly budgeting period. Your budget allows for emergency savings (3-6 months' worth of monthly expenses), retirement savings (a minimum of two percent of your after-tax income), and personal financial goals. Your budget records real and goal sums as a foundation for subsequent review. Try using digital/online resources to make budgeting more convenient.

You can now recognize that there are two methods you can use when creating a budget. The first is a personal approach, and the second is a company-wide approach.

I'll discuss both approaches here, but since the personal approach is our primary focus, let's start with that.

## Understanding A Personal Budget And Why Should You Care

In this case, the budget is a financial plan that allocates future personal income to expenses, savings, and debt payment. In other words, the personal budget is a document where the income and expenses of money that a person expects to have in a given period are quantified. Past expenses and personal debt must be taken into account when creating this budget.

### 1. Not Having One

Spending without a budget is the most serious financial mistake you can make. Suppose you don't make a monthly spending schedule. In that case, you're either living in between financial crises or, at the very least, you're overspending in a way that would place you in debt. You're probably not putting money aside for essential financial goals like a home or retirement.

Even though you might be able to get by, for the time being, you would not be able to move on if you do not build a budget despite this budgeting snafu. If the idea of itemizing a laundry list of monthly expenditures is deterring you from creating a budget, concentrate on one or two spending categories in your first budget to keep it straightforward.

### 2. Guessing at Monthly Costs

To create a monthly budget that helps you live within your means, you must calculate your overall monthly income and expenditures in different categories.

However, you do not know how much to allocate to the various spending categories in your budget, such as lodging, transportation, and food, until you build your first budget. As a result, you may make the common budgeting mistake of estimating your monthly expenses based on guesswork, which can cause you to underestimate or overestimate your spending drastically. For example, let's assume that you allocate $200 for groceries when you usually spend about $500 per month. Your budget would almost certainly collapse if you cut $300 from your food budget.

Instead of guessing, log all of your spending for a month in different categories and use the totals as a benchmark when creating your budget. Reduce the expenses steadily over the next few months.

### 3. Assigning Expenses by Paycheck

You could be allocating specific expenses to each paycheck, whether you're paying weekly or biweekly. This budgeting blunder could mean that money is tight the week you pay your mortgage or rent, particularly if you have many bills due at the same time.

Rather than allocating an entire paycheck to the most significant expense and leaving little room for other expenses, set aside money from each paycheck to cover different cost categories. Suppose you obey the 50/ 30/ 20 budgeting law, for example. In that case, you should set aside 5o% of your income for housing and other "needs," 30% for "wants" like vacations, and 20% for savings and debt payments.

You can also set aside a month's worth of earnings to use for your monthly budget and then use the remainder of your earnings to pay for next month's bills. This process makes budgeting easier and helps prevent frequent cash flow problems that can force you to cut spending in vital categories like groceries or even make late payments on bills.

4. **Not Tracking Your Spending**

- Monitoring your expenses means keeping track of your outgoings during the month, preferably regularly. You risk overspending and blowing your budget too fast if you don't track your spending or spending too little and struggling to reach financial targets like debt reduction if you don't track your spending. The explanation for this is because if you don't know when you've achieved anything, you won't know when you've hit your cap.

- Finding an expense-tracking tool that works for you, whether it's a spreadsheet, software, or good old-fashioned pen and paper, is the secret. When you start monitoring your spending, you'll be able to hold yourself accountable to stay on track, recognize common budgeting mistakes like overspending, and correct the habits that contribute to them.
- Try using the envelope method of budgeting if you have trouble managing your money during the month. You split the money for spending into several envelopes, each with a different spending category.

### 5. Leaving Out Items

Another common blunder is failing to account for all of one's planned expenditures in one's budget. Small regular costs, such as your everyday subway trip, or even significant one-time expenses, such as wedding and holiday presents, may be left out.

If you don't account for an expense, no matter how small or infrequently you incur it, you've made a financial error that might throw your budget off in the month you pay for it.

- Divide the sum you usually pay for irregular expenditures, including car insurance, by 12 and set aside the money per month in your budget.
- Include trim, often overlooked budget items as well.
- You should recognize any expenditures that you lack after a few months of budgeting and change your allotment for the following month accordingly.

### 6. Not Working as a Team

Spending in a silo is one of the most common budgeting traps for couples to avoid. For example, you and your spouse both finish in the same category at the same time of the month; your combined expenses will surpass what you expected to spend in that category, causing you to overspend and blow your budget accidentally. Alternatively, one partner can neglect the other's particular financial needs and desires. This practice will ultimately lead to both individuals abandoning the budget.

You and your partner should talk about where you are financially and where you want to be regularly and work on a budget together. This will prevent you from overspending and keep you on track to meet individual and joint financial goals.

### 7. Not Having an Emergency Fund

An emergency fund is funds set aside to cover unforeseen costs such as medical bills or home repairs. The fund should be adequate to cover three to six months of living costs.

If you lack this financial safety net, you may have to dig into your long-term savings to pay your bills, or, even worse, and you may end up in debt by depending on credit. If you keep an emergency fund, you can use it when you need it and then replenish it so that it's usable when you need it again.

You must, however, prepare for it like you would any other financial target. You intend to contribute to your emergency fund as a fixed cost in your budget's saving category when you're creating it, including the monthly number.

This strategy will hold you responsible for saving and keep you on track to accumulating a good emergency fund.

### 8. Not Budgeting for Fun

Depriving yourself of all entertainment expenses is a budgeting pitfall that increases the chances of blowing your monthly budget. Watching a movie, going to see your favorite artist in concert, and even occasional shopping sprees are all acceptable as long as you include them in your monthly budget and adhere to the amount you set aside. Or, you end up paying more than you would have if the regulations had not been put in place.

### 9. Classifying Wants as Needs

Another common budgeting mistake is confusing "wants," which are non-essential expenses such as personal travel or dining out, with "needs," which are required expenses such as mortgage payments and groceries.

Misclassifying wants as needs or lumping them together under the same budget group can be financially risky because you're unlikely to cut back on needs as much as wants. To avoid falling into this budgeting trap, analyze each of the things you consider essentials and ask yourself if you could survive without them. If "yes," the object is a non-essential cost and should be treated as a want.

### 10. Assuming Your Monthly Bills Are Set

Fixed expenditures are also seen as non-negotiable budget items by many people. Your cable or cell phone bill, for example, could be the same every month. Consequently, when looking at your budget, you do not look for ways to save money regularly.

This is a common budgeting mistake that can lead to budget bloat if you choose to use overpriced service providers year after year. Consider downgrading to a more competitive package or calling in to negotiate a lower monthly price if your service provider is excellent. If you're ready to make a change, compare prices for everything from insurance to cable and gym memberships to get the most bang for your buck. You could save tens or hundreds of dollars per month by doing

# The Steps To Setting Up Your Personal Budget

It would be best if you established a series of financial goals. These can be anything from wanting to save for your children's university to want to pay you a trip around the world. To fulfill your goals (and perhaps your dreams), you must take into account a series of considerations that we are going to list below:

Every so often, you should look at your budget and analyze it again to see if you are meeting your goals. You must do it often to know that you are on the right track, But you don't have to do it every day.

To achieve what you want, it is best to set goals regularly. So you will see how you improve over time. It would be best if you thought in the short and long term. You can achieve goals quickly, but others, such as retirement plans, are long-term. You must take this into account. Do not budget too tightly, as it will most likely be too challenging to follow, and in the end, you will end up quitting. You better be realistic. Patience is very wise.

### 1. Make A Budget to Start Investing.

One of the reasons for having a budget on hand is that it helps you know the amount of money you have saved. Having a good cushion of money is a good thing. However, if you don't do anything with it, it loses value over time. That is why it is recommended to invest it so that it generates profits.

One of the advantages of investing is that you don't have to do a lot to make

money grow. The truth is that it is a mixture of knowing the product in which it is invested and luck

### 2. Applications to Create Your Budget

Pocket guard. This application can generate a general budget automatically based on your spending habits, apart from other functions.

You'll be able to track your spending and budget to save more money. To keep track of all your expenses, you may link the application to your bank account.

### 3. What To Keep In Mind When Making A Budget

Once the personal budget is made, you mustn't spend more money than you enter.

- If you have small expenses, you can make a section of "others" instead of making a long list. In it, you can add these.
- When you have the budget made, it is vital to control the expenses you make in leisure. If you limit yourself, you will have money that you can use to buy things you need at the end of the month.
- Finally, you are the one who determines how you want to build your budget, so you are not obligated to obey anything we say in this article to the letter. What counts is that you stick to the underlying principle.

## 4. Tips for Planning Your Budget

- Save all receipts so that you can verify their history in your bank account and try to reduce the number of expenses in your first budget. If you think you are spending too much, look at all the expenses you have. Sure there are some of these that you can eliminate or reduce at least.
- If you can save money, it may be best that you start to get performance with this.

- Always try to save a mattress for any unforeseen expenses. When you find yourself in an emergency, you will be glad to have this mattress.
- Always write down any unexpected expenses you may have. This way, you will not have to borrow money, so you will not have to face debt, and you will save yourself headaches.

## 5. Steps to Create your Goals

### Step 1: Set Goals

Before you can begin to manage your money, you need to identify what is important to you. Then you have a foundation to decide what you want to do with your money. Write down what is important to you and use your list to help you determine goals for your money. A short—term goal might be to pay off debt or buy a new appliance. A medium-term goal may be to take a cruise or save the down—payment for a new car. Long—term goals typically include retirement plans, paying off a home, or helping children start independently.

The goals you set are yours; you have the power to choose what is important to you and design your goals accordingly. Most people's money problems occur because they don't clearly know what they want to do with their money and therefore spend it randomly. Clear goals are the targets you are aiming for and help you build your plan. After that, it's a simple process to map out how you will achieve your financial goals.

When setting financial goals, think about how much you need to save and for how long. Then think about how you will accomplish those savings. For most people, this means putting a set amount aside each month, according to their pay schedule. This monthly amount is the difference between just having a wish... or making your wish a reality.

Be realistic when setting your goals. You can always increase your savings later, but start by planning for success! It can be strangely motivating to see your plans in black and white, so take some time to write down your financial goals on the next page.

## Step 2: Identify Income and Expenses

After you've set some financial goals for yourself, it's time to examine where your money comes from and where it goes right now. It's quick to fall into bad habits when it comes to money management. Some money management habits are beneficial and encourage us to reap benefits in the future. Others are pessimistic and can lead us astray. Begin by compiling a list of all of your household's income sources and amounts. Include all regular income, including salaries (after taxes), commissions, self-employment income, child tax benefits, pensions, child care and spousal assistance, and other regular income.

This can be challenging because most people know where their money comes from but are less confident of where it goes. Spending covers everything you spend your money on, not only what you would think of as "expenses" (utility bills, groceries, commuting costs), but also rainy-day investments, mortgage payments, life insurance premiums, and RRSP donations.

If you keep track of your family's spending, this is a good place to start. Since many households do not keep track of their expenses, you will need to collect spending data from bank account or credit card statements, cheque register books, receipts, or bills.

Any of our expenses are on a weekly or monthly basis, such as car fuel, groceries, and utility bills.

Seasonal or annual expenditures, such as presents, vet costs, holidays, home maintenance, new glasses, or clothes, must also be factored into our budget. Simply divide the amount you pay per year on these things by 12 to determine monthly sums for your annual expenses.

Looking back and finding costs is a good place to start. You may have noted, though, that there seems to be more money going out than you have records for. That's because every family has spending "leakage" — small expenses that go unnoticed but add up.

It cannot always be simple, and you may forget to record some things. However, monitoring is a critical component of determining your expenses. When you first start tracking, you will be tempted to watch how much money you believe you should be investing. Avoid doing so because the results would not accurately represent your expenses. Now is the time to figure out what you're doing with your money right now; there will be time later to make changes and decisions when you get ready to put your strategy into effect. Do your best; you may be shocked by what you discover.

## Step 3: Separate Needs from Wants

As people track their spending, they discover that some of their money gets used for things they really don't need. Instead, they merely want them and often buy them impulsively. Impulse spending is unplanned spending, purchasing things that you may or may not need, or spending more on an item than you'd planned.

People spend impulsively for a variety of reasons. If they're in a good mood, they spend out of pleasure and keep a good mood. If they're in a bad mood, they spend to try and make themselves feel better. Some people spend in certain places or at certain times because they feel obligated to do so, e.g., on vacation, during special holiday seasons, when they're with certain people, or while engaging in specific activities. Impulse spending habits are often linked to stress levels. A little stress can be motivating, but a lot of stress can rob you of your ability to make wise choices between needs and wants. If you would like to learn more about why you spend impulsively and what you can do to change your spending patterns, please request a copy of the Credit Counselling Society's handout, Impulse Spending.

The key to good money management is separating needs from wants. If you aren't sure if an item is a need or a want, do without it for some time. If after that time you truly can't live without it, it may be a need. However, even the essentials like shelter or transportation involve a want vs. need calculation. For instance, you may have evaluated all possible transportation methods for you to get to work and determined that you need to purchase a car. Fine, but which car you buy is another choice you make. Do you buy the more expensive SUV that you want, or will a less expensive, more economical vehicle meet your need? Almost everything you buy involves a want vs. need determination, and ultimately, how you make these choices will determine if you reach your goals or not.

You can have almost anything you want; you just can't afford everything you want.

**Step 4: Design Your Budget**

Many people dislike the word "budget" because it connotes constraints, deprivation, and a lack of funds to spend on enjoyable activities. Relax, your budget is your spending plan — it will help you live within your means, escape the burden of financial problems, and give you the ability to make decisions based on what you have. Most significantly, a budget will help you set out a strategy for achieving your objectives.

Until proceeding, you must ensure that your expenditures do not exceed your revenue. This is the point at which you must make certain decisions based on what you discovered when you monitored your spending and isolated your needs from your wants. Expenses include all of your spending, not just your bills. The money you put into your children's RESP is considered an expense. Money saved in savings accounts for a holiday next year is often considered an expense. Savings may be the furthest thing from your mind if you are facing financial difficulties, but you must intend to have money for the unexpected even during this period. Saving money is the difference between making a budget that works and one that doesn't. It not only protects you from financial catastrophe but also assists you in meeting your financial objectives.

People who have funds set aside to cover living expenses and seasonal expenses in the event of an emergency do not need to rely on credit that they may not be able to repay. If your salary changes, your emergency savings will cover your basic living expenses. For example, in the event of a work loss, it normally takes three months to get back on track with either a new source of income or outside assistance. During this time, you would also need funds for rent, groceries, and other necessities; this is where your emergency savings will come in handy. If you have a large car or home repair bill, you will have emergency savings to cover it. Using income tax refunds, unexpected bonuses, or gift money to fund an emergency savings account will help you start.

In addition to emergency savings, you should have general savings that you can use to achieve your financial goals and ensure your financial security in the future. Some people call this "paying yourself first." This savings is for the seasonal expenditures as well as your priorities that you listed in your budget. The easiest way to save money is to set it away before you need it. Speak with your bank or credit union about setting up automatic transfers to savings accounts any time you get paid.

Thank you so much! You've built a balanced budget by preparing your resources for the month and distinguishing needs from wants. You've set your goals and determined how much money you'll need to set aside for seasonal and unforeseen expenses. It's now time to bring the strategy into effect.

Return to your budget and make a list of all of your fixed, cash/variable, and savings expenses.

Fixed expenses are the same amount every month on the same day — they do not adjust. Rent/mortgage, insurance, and bank fees are a few examples.

Cash/variable expenses occur every month, but the sum varies, and they occur on various days. Groceries, gas, and entertainment are a few examples.

Savings expenses are funds set aside for later use. They include saving for unforeseen/seasonal costs, emergencies, and long-term goals.

Add all of the fixed costs together. Divide these by 2 whether you are paying semimonthly or biweekly. This is the sum you would deduct from each paycheck to fulfill your monthly obligations. This money should be held in a separate account (fixed expenses account) where money is transferred regularly (bi-weekly, semi-monthly, or monthly), and expenses are deducted automatically. You should not use this account for anything. Rep this move for all of your Savings (S) expenses.

## Step 5: Put Your Plan into Action

Add up all of your Cash/Variable (C) expenses and then divide these by **4** so that you have a weekly amount (you can divide by **2** so that you have money to cover **2** weeks of expenses, it's your choice). You can take the money as cash or keep it in a separate bank account from your fixed expenses, knowing that once the money is gone, it's gone until you pay yourself again (weekly, bi-weekly, semi-monthly, or monthly).

## Step 6: Manage Seasonal and Irregular Expenses

The next step is to plan and save for seasonal and irregular expenses. Keep updating your tracker, so you know where your money is going. Seasonal and irregular expenses are those items that show up in your budget but do not occur monthly. The frequency of these expenses could be every few months, every 6 months, or even annually.

Open up a savings account for seasonal and irregular expenses

Add up all of your seasonal and irregular expenses for the whole year (seasonal and irregular expenses).

Divide the total amount of annual seasonal and irregular expenses by the number of paydays you have in 1 year. For example, suppose your annual seasonal and irregular expenses total $1800, and you get paid every 2 weeks. In that case, you'll divide $1800 by 26 paydays, which equals nearly $7o/pay cheque.

Start transferring over the set amount every payday into your seasonal and irregular expenses savings account.

When a seasonal or irregular expense comes up, transfer the funds from your savings account to your checking account and pay your bill.

Track your expenses, so you know what to plan for, for next year.

# CHAPTER THREE

# Analyzing Your Income And Expenditure

One of the key steps of budgeting is to Analyze your own expenditure and income. This chapter looks at those topics.

## The Importance Of Tracking Your Income And Expenditure

One of the most important aspects of making your budget work is keeping track of your expenses. You can't say you've spent more if you don't know how much you've spent each month. Even small expenses can cause your budget to blow. There are several options available to keep track of your expenses. One of the simplest is a written accounting or tracking system. It may be even simpler to select budgeting software that integrates with a phone expense tracking app.

This will give you the chance to keep up to date while on the go. It is also essential to know how to keep track of your expenses in a notebook. This can also help you be more aware of what is going on and where you are spending it. It can assist you in identifying the areas where you need to change.

**Here are reasons why you should be tracking your personal expenses.**

If you own a small business, you have probably considered just about everything products, marketing, and a thousand other considerations. Many small business owners, on the other hand, overlook their expenses. You must keep track of how much money you have in the bank and what you're doing with it if you want to succeed in business.

- Beginning planning and following costs is a substantial initial step, yet it will do almost no great if you don't keep it up. It would be ideal if you checked your financial plan regularly and spent at least a small amount of time every day
- checking your receipts and recording costs.

- For what reason is it so crucial to track your costs? If you know what your costs and benefits are, you'll be able to predict whether you'll be in a financial bind early on. Like this, you can make a move to take care of the issue before it's past the point of no return.

**Following your costs assists you with seeing spending botches before they become grievous individual accounting issues.**

Being wild isn't something anyone would strive for when it comes to their personal budget. Nothing is more frustrating financially than feeling as though you don't know what's going on with your money.

Overspending is perhaps the most convincing reason why people end up in financial trouble. Individuals develop a daily habit of spending as much as (or more than) they earn. As a result, it becomes difficult to achieve any long-term financial targets, and any unexpected events can be surprising. In fact, barely less than 80% of US laborers live to work.

While it's easy to point out a few large expenses that contribute to overspending, it's often a slew of minor expenses that are the real culprit. It is not difficult to select the $1oo cost; however, 1.0 prices of $io will frequently leave a lot of notice. It's just $io, all things considered, but it can easily add up if $1.0 happens repeatedly.

Following your expenses will reveal a wide range of overspending. If you stick with it, cost tracking will help you identify a small problem until it becomes a more serious problem where you're struggling to make ends meet.

The breaking news is that you are making an effort to document every monetary transaction you make; you are fundamental, steering on everything without exception, including your money. You will be aware of how much cash is in your ledger and how much you have available to spend at every given time. As a result, when you track your expenses, you take full responsibility for your accounts.

**Cost following gives the spine to a proper and reasonable spending plan.**

Numerous individuals partner "monetary duty" with "making an individual financial plan." Still, an incredible functional financial plan is based on top of your spending's exact image, which you can just make through following your costs. Everybody has distinctive ways of managing money and schedules, and basically, thudding an instant spending plan on top of your propensities will quite often bring about calamity.

All things being equal, sensible spending begins by investigating how you've been going through your cash, arranging that spending into reasonable classifications, and defining some humble objectives for a portion of the more adaptable classes.

For instance, if you burn through $200 on your leisure activities every month, $150 is reasonable to add up to that class's financial plan. Yet, you don't have the foggiest idea of the amount you're spending – and in this way the amount to spending plan – without following your costs en-route. Realizing your genuine spending allows you to make sensible spending numbers that can help you gain positive monetary headway.

**Following your expenses helps make you more aware of expenditure at the time.**

When you start following your costs, you'll see that the cycle makes you more aware of the spending decisions you make for the day. You'll begin to relate things like, say, that $5 stop at the coffeehouse with the effect it has on your total spending toward the month's end, and that will propel you to track down a less expensive arrangement or to scale back a propensity that genuinely adds up.

It's straightforward redundancy. The more occasions you take a gander at and consider a specific kind of cost and the enormous effect it's having on you, the more probable you are to think about that cost with a more basic eye.

This doesn't imply that the following costs will make you never burn through cash on anything fun until the end of time. All things being equal, it will make you more aware of those costs. There may be times where you remember you're not getting a ton of significant worth out of a treat, yet on different occasions, it's genuinely worth your time and energy.

Considering yourself responsible, following your costs on an everyday premise helps you see your improvement making progress toward your monetary objectives. Without a doubt, there might be times when you need to reply to yourself for a wrong economic choice, yet monitoring your positive advancement is comparably significant.

Consider the big picture; if you have an objective of saving $25,000 in a year and track your costs each day, you can praise every one of the little successes enrooted. For example, if you decide to skip a pricey dinner out and instead cook at home, tracking your expenses will allow you to see the impact of that decision on your investment funds goal. Keeping tabs on your development assists with keeping you inspired while in transit to your objectives.

**It may aid in the improvement of your relationship with your partner.**

Cash is perhaps the most well-known wellsprings of debates among couples, and it frequently comes down to ways of managing money. When one partner spends more on frills than the other, it can quickly become irritating, especially if the extra spending is causing other financial issues.

Following your costs is an effective method to get a clearer perspective on your spending vulnerable sides and give accommodating data in case discussions. A detailed record of where the cash went can diminish a "he said/she said" dynamic down to real numbers.

While, it can't settle every monetary question, it can go far toward assisting the two accomplices with recognizing spending issues without falling back on allegations and outrage.

**Following your costs can execute monetary pressure.**

Perhaps the main monetary pressure hotspots for the vast majority are the interminable inquiry of where the cash's entirety went. A check comes in, and it appears as though you're flush with money; however, a couple of days pass, and the record looks unfilled. What was the deal? Following your costs responds to that question.

Following entirety of your costs implies you know where each dime of your cash is going, and that changes the inquiry from an upsetting secret to something clear and justifiable. As opposed to feeling like everything is wild, it changes the investigation into individual dynamics, which is undeniably less distressing.

Obliviousness in individual accounting is not ecstasy; we've all seen those individuals that simply don't know appear to think often about their ways of managing money. They toss every buy on an alternate Mastercard, money spit and span vehicles that they can't bear, and wind up covered under a pile of monetary pressure.

The entirety of this can be maintained a strategic distance from with **2** fundamental advances: living on a tight spending plan and following your costs every day.

The more persevering and restrained you are tied in with following your costs, the more outlandish you will settle on absurd monetary choices. What's more, as you decrease your ridiculous economic decisions, you will lessen one of the primary sources of pressure in your life: cash issues.

So, following your costs returns a feeling of authority over your funds to you. You're not, at this point, only curious to see what happens on a monetary thrill ride.

**It makes it a lot simpler to set monetary objectives.**

Suppose you go weeks, or worse, months, without checking your ledger and entering your expenses into a spending plan. In that case, you are jeopardizing your financial stability. Consider the probability that someone steals your check card information and begins robbing your bank. That is not a situation in which you can seek the most difficult solution.

Consider this: would you rather have a fake trade in your financial balance the day it happens or find someone who spent all of your money after your lease search ricochets?

Following your expenses, each day is a small price to pay for your financial stability. The final advantage of tracking your expenses is that it makes it much easier to set financial goals for yourself.

You can unquestionably set direct spending objectives for yourself, limiting your spending on a particular diversion to $50 per month. This is analogous to planning, which is simply a form of a goal-oriented economic environment.

In either case, the true advantage of identifying spending goals in this manner is that meeting such goals frees up money for more important monetary purposes in daily life. Assume you can handle $200 a month from your expenses on a few different schools. You have $200 per month to make up for missed time with your bills, avoid overdraft periods, set up a just-in-case account, and begin squaring away the high-interest debt. It's related to keeping track of your accounts. Following your costs is usually simple, to begin with.

The simplest way to get started is to simply document all of your expenses in a journal. You only need a small winding note pad and a pen. Start by keeping track of your expenses with a simple pocket scratch pad and a pen. If you spend money on something, you can write it down quickly on the scratchpad or stuff a receipt in the notepad pages.

At any point, you burn through cash, save the receipt, and once or twice a year, record everything you burn through cash on the date, the thing, and the amount. You can (and should) classify it as well. You may think it's easy to use categories like "food," but you can go a step further and use classifications like "important food," "eating out," and "luxurious cuisine" to differentiate between needs and different types of requirements.

When recording prices, go through staple documents and use a highlighter to categorize everything into "fundamental food," "exquisite cuisine," (food at the supermarket that had a less costly alternative), and "family supplies." Do the same for all multi-item receipts. Connect another item called "Food at the store" with the classification "important food" and the aggregate. Another thing is called "Food at the supermarket" with the class "exquisite cuisine." Then another thing is called "Supplies at supermarket" with the class "family supplies." Each has the total cost of those stuff from the receipt.

There isn't a good list of classifications with which to organize your expenses. Just make up some that sound amazing to you. You will just need to start thinking about them now and leave a room for classifications; when you have two or three dozen passages, devise classes and order the costs.

You discover that there is a lot of value in doing this by hand. It will help you keep track of your expenses in ways that merely typing information into computerized instruments will not; finding devices that automatically fill in the information might be even less important for you. They are still helpful. When it comes to mechanized instruments, there are devices prescribed based on how you choose to move toward things; you may not use any of these consistently, mostly because you feel awkward using outsider apparatuses to get to your monetary records directly; however, this is not because they're untrustworthy at all; you may very well decide to limit the number of online stores y

Mint, which consequently recovers information from your documents and displays it in an application, is the easiest to use — nevertheless, it feels the most uninvolved and least welcoming to me. It's simple and free to use; however, you'll notice that it expends a lot of effort in providing you with ideas.

A far superior option is a membership administration called You Need a Budget, which you can seriously consider as the best comprehensive automated planning and cost-following instrument available. It also recovers information for you; however, you can enter a lot of data yourself to improve it, and it provides a ton of valuable insights into your data.

If you're a bookkeeping page nerd, I'd recommend Tiller cash, which integrates with Google Sheets to automatically move details from your records into an accounting page.

When you have a little bit of detail, you can start making some fantastic decisions. The true engagement of cost recording is something remarkable. It serves as a strong, reliable indicator of where your money is heading, and it can influence your intuition as you document it.

However, when you begin to compile a large amount of spending data, it becomes much more impressive. The data you've gathered allows you to take a step back and consider your longer-term spending plans.

With a month of information from following your spending, you can undoubtedly pose inquiries like, "How much cash did I spend a month ago at cafes?" or

"How much cash did I spend a month ago eating out?" or "How much cash did I spend a month ago on amusement buys?" The responses to those inquiries — and many like them, contingent upon the classes you've picked — can shape your reasoning regarding spending decisions.

The acknowledgment that you're going through hundreds per month at restaurants, $1,000 somewhat recently eating out at fine eateries, or $350 on leisure activities can be a genuine shocker. In addition to the fact that it shows you where your cash is going, it can likewise help you understand that your money is going towards things that aren't giving a ton of significant worth in your life for the sum you're spending.

When you include your spending in every class for the month, what you're doing is making a spending's spine. You can go through those classes, sort out which ones are sensible and which ones will be ones where you're overspending and can scale back, and afterward utilize those real numbers to make an essential spending plan for yourself.

This entire cycle uncovers a significant truth about planning. The genuine benefit of planning isn't in making slick outlines and tables yet in the way that it can recognize a couple of your most noticeably awful spending regions and assist you with overseeing them. It's not in an outline but instead in how that graph changes your conduct.

For the vast majority, spending will uncover a few territories of overspending on trivial things, which you can scale back by decision, just as certain zones of total expenditure that you'd prefer to scale back (like managing bills). While bringing in more cash is consistently an excellent answer for this issue, it is anything but a prompt arrangement; along these lines, the brisk device close by is moderation.

One great approach to begin is by managing your necessary month-to-month bills. Here are 40 strategies for managing your customary month-to-month accounts, just as some average bills that individuals can erase. Find out if each charge you have is essential and, on the off chance that it is, ask yourself how you can scale that bill back a bit. A phenomenal initial step is to call that organization and see how it can be dealt with to make that bill more modest.

The other methodology is to scale back your excessive spending. I must believe it's an ill-conceived notion to slice unnecessary spending deep down. If you trim out the entirety of the stuff you appreciate, you will detest the progressions rapidly. All things being equal, you should attempt to distinguish the 20% (or something like that) of your unimportant spending that is least imperative to you and cut those things while being aware of what you're acquiring because of those cuts. If you spend $400 a month eating out, see if you can reduce that to $300 by cutting out the $100 you spend on the most forgettable suppers. If you have some cost, you simply don't have any desire to cut, search for some other expense you can scale back somewhat more confounded.

Following your costs takes a touch of time; however, it's an excellent prod toward more intelligent spending and better monetary decisions.

Following your spending is probably the best thing to begin doing during your financial turnaround. It will you a little consistent push to try not to burn through cash on little things and, before long, uncover a portion of your most noticeably awful ways of managing money. Understanding this essential in your life will abstain from overspending — and just knowing where the entirety of the cash was going — this will be a groundbreaking change in your monetary life.

After you develop a few sections, begin taking a gander at the examples and see what they're informing you concerning reasonable changes you can make to your spending. It requires some investment. However, it can massively affect your utilization of cash.

## What Are The Income And Expenses In Personal Budget?

**Salary.** If you have a fixed salary, you must indicate this. On the other hand, if you are self-employed and your income varies from month to month, you should put the lowest. If your partner enters an amount each month, it should also be noted in the budget. It is also vital you put down the extra income.

You must note if you have a pension or sickness compensation. In the case of illness, you only have to enter the current compensation period, not the one you think you will have.

Whether you're on maternity or paternity leave, you'll need to work that into your budget as well. If you receive any scholarships for studies. If you have another house that you are renting, it must also appear in the income section of the budget.

You have another type of income, either selling items periodically or possible benefits that you receive from the government.

There are quite a few types of monthly expenses for a person that you should be aware of. You must write them in your budget. Since there are quite a few, we have decided to show them to you in different categories to have them more transparent.

**Accommodation Costs**

- If you are paying rent, you must enter the expenses of this here.
- If you are paying a mortgage, you should also write down these expenses.
- The cost of electricity. Being expenses that can change every month, you should look at how much you paid the previous year and the average.

- Payment for water. As in the previous case, it is best to look at the average of what you spent previously.
- House insurance expenses.
- Community expenses, if any.

**Car Expenses**

- The cost of the loan debt. In other words, the payments that you still have to face.
- The taxes that may be on the cars.
- The insurance car.
- The fuel. You have to calculate more or less what you spend each month on gasoline. You can do it by making a monthly average of the last six months, for example.
- The costs of repairs and maintenance (such as changing the oil or the brake pad). To find out what it costs, you can call the mechanic to find out.

The expense for parking. Either in the parking lot next to your house or other parking lots. It is good that you make an average calculation of how much you will spend per month.

- The possible tire changes. Even if you believe it is unlikely, you should consider it.
- The inspection of the car. This is usually mandatory for older vehicles.

**Fixed Expenses**

- Any insurance you have, such as medical insurance, home insurance or some
- insurance for your children.
- If you have someone to take care of your children when working, for example, a
- babysitter.
- The mobile rate.
- The subscription to the gym.
- Bank charges.
- If you have a pension plan.

**Household Expenses**

- All food. We emphasize the word "all" since we also count sweets, ice cream, or tacos.
- Lunch or coffee expenses if you eat away from home.
- All products related to hygiene and beauty. Examples of these products can be soap, shampoo, deodorant, pants, toothpaste, or makeup.

- Laundry detergents, fabric softeners detergents, bath towels, kitchen dishes, and utensils.
- The clothes and shoes.
- The new furniture or appliances that you should buy if the ones you already have broken down.
- Possible expenses for visits to the doctor, dentist, and medicines that doctors can prescribe. To get an idea you can look at what you spent on this aspect last year.
- Any leisure or fun. It can be from sports activities, books, dinners, trips abroad, or drinks in bars.
- Other expenses can be, for example, including birthday and Christmas in this category.

## The Difference Between Fixed And Variable Expense

Fixed expenses are costs that you can predict with certainty for personal budgeting purposes because they do not vary from month to month or period to period. They appear to consume the most of your budget because they include rent or mortgage payments, car payments, and insurance premiums. Variable costs, on the other hand, are difficult to predict before they occur. You can predict them, but there is a chance that they will be higher or lower than you anticipated. Groceries, gas, and electricity are a few examples. As these examples demonstrate, while discretionary expenditure is often a variable cost, variable expenditures may also be necessities.

It is important to understand the fixed and variable costs to create an accurate and practical budget. If you still have cash flow issues while earning a decent income, a financial planner will assist you.

1. **What Are Fixed Expenses?**

Car payments, mortgage or rent payments, insurance premiums, and real estate taxes are examples of common fixed expenses. Typically, these costs are unchangeable. On the plus hand, they are simple to budget for since they are generally consistent and are paid regularly. Some fixed costs, such as a gym membership or a video service subscription, can be discretionary.

And if these bills are consistent per month, you can be able to reduce their costs. If you have a monthly subscription that you seldom use, there might be a cheaper alternative plan. Try a lower-cost gym subscription or a different video service, for example. To save even more money, shop around for alternative auto insurance, health insurance, life insurance, and homeowners or renters insurance policies.

When you reduce your fixed costs, you save more money each month or pay period. This is because fixed costs typically consume the greatest portion of your budget. As a result, when you reduce your fixed costs, you reduce the amount of your budget that is allocated to them. This is a perfect alternative to cutting back on other expenses, such as purchasing new clothing or ordering takeout. Saving even a small amount on your fixed expenses will quickly add up.

For example, if you pay $1,100 a month instead of $1,185, the quality of your apartment and neighborhood cannot improve significantly. However, the $85 per month would grow to $1,020 over a year. What's the best part? You just need to make the cost-cutting decision once to reap the benefits.

## 2. What Are Variable Expenses?

Variable costs can be thought of as the sum total of your everyday spending decisions. Do you buy traditional or organic fruits and vegetables? Do you go to Starbucks or make your own coffee? However, not all contingent costs are discretionary. Variable expenses are so named because the amount you pay varies from month to month.

While variable costs are frequently discretionary expenses, some may be needed. Buying gas for your car each month and car repairs and maintenance is a variable cost. Shopping for groceries is another variable cost. Utility bills may also be considered variable costs since they vary from month to month. For example, you will spend more money on electricity in July than you do in December because of air conditioning.

Since, they affect your lifestyle, variable expenses can be more difficult to reduce than fixed expenses. You might have to choose between cooking and ordering takeout. Or maybe you have to choose between buying new clothes and watching a new movie. Cutting back on variable expenses takes more willpower daily than cutting back on fixed expenses.

### 3. Looking At Your Financial Habits

Many of your variable expenses may turn out to be reasonably predictable. You could see a trend if you go through the previous year's credit and debit card statements. For example, let's say you get your hair cut every four weeks. Will you, however, make a haircut last six weeks? That would save you approximately three haircuts at $30 each, for a total savings of $90.

You may also use data from the previous year to predict how much you usually spend on different types of variable expenses. You might, for example, have a grocery category, a utility category, and a travel expenses category.

Next, take the amount you spent in these categories in the previous year and divide it by 12. Then, for each variable cost, you can set aside the amount each month. You could also open separate savings accounts for each variable expense category if you wanted. This will help you see how much money you have left to spend on each category each month. It can also convert variable expenses into expenses that can be anticipated and budgeted each month, similar to fixed expenses.

In addition, keep track of the fixed expenditures. You should prepare ahead of time if the insurance premiums are going to rise in the coming year. Cancel any monthly services you were unaware you were already paying for. Keeping track of monthly fees will help you avoid paying for services you don't use.

Creating and sticking to a budget can often be as simple as a few clever tricks. While it may be easier in principle to reduce variable costs, it may be easier in practice to reduce fixed costs. This is because it is more difficult to reverse a decision after it has become ingrained in your lifestyle. Furthermore, it does not feel like a loss, while cutting back on your fun spending most likely would. Reduced fixed costs result in automatic, non-optional savings. You will not only be able to free up money to pay down debt or save for the future, but you will not have to give up as much of your current lifestyle.

## What To Do If Your Expense Exceeds Your Budget

- You've lost your work.
- You have a huge unanticipated cost.
- Your way of life creeps up on you without your knowledge.
- Suddenly, you find yourself in a vacuum. Your monthly expenses surpass your profits, and you're gripped by a sense of fear, desperation, and panic. Often it is our fault, and other times it is a result of circumstances beyond our control.

Whatever the reason, action must be taken to keep your head above water because drowning is not an option—it is not your course. Credit cards are one of the most common places where we get into trouble. Nothing beats whipping out the plastic and putting off the pain—but therein lies the pit. It seems to be easier to continue to sustain your lifestyle while in debt than to change your lifestyle. The prospect of a new career, a bonus, an inheritance, a lottery win, or, if things get very bad, a loan from your 401(k) plan—all risky things to depend on. You'll be in a debt loop before you know it.

Another issue is lifestyle creep. You spend your well-earned increase on more expensive toys, more expensive holidays, and more regular "extras." If any adjustments arise that hurt your profits, you will likely find yourself in a difficult situation. Unless you track your spending by category, it's difficult to identify the culprits before the scales tip. So, what do you do when you realize you're in big trouble? Here's where you shouldn't begin: Investigate bankruptcy or firms that will approach your credit card companies to try to restructure your debt. Your dilemma will not be solved by blaming and shaming. Your tenacity is needed to get yourself back on track.

**Here's What To Do:**

- **Evaluate and Analyze**- Before you can do something helpful, you must first assess the situation. Take the time to examine your financial situation, including your net worth (assets minus debt) and cash flow (money in vs. money out). Make a list of everything.
- **Break down-** Once you've gathered the big numbers, divide them into basic categories (how much you spend on food, clothing, rent,

credit card payments, loans, entertainment, insurance, personal care, vacations, etc.).

- **Cut-** Trim the fat. If it is not contractually required or necessary to live (for example, food), get rid of it. There will be no excuses. Rent/mortgage, loans, and credit card fees are also contractual obligations that must be met.
- **Decide-** To get your financial life back on track, you must take decisive steps. Your decision to live within your means is critical to getting through this difficult period. This will allow you to sleep through the night more quickly.

For many people, cutting discretionary expenditures is enough to get their budget back into balance. Yes, it is painful to part from the treats to which you have become accustomed. However, often a reset is needed to bring awareness and a new point of view. According to behavioral finance studies, we are most in touch with our present feelings, and thinking about suffering from the past feels remote and difficult to place.

So, if we are feeling bad right now, it is difficult to remember feeling good. However, like the stock market, our lives follow a non-linear path;

successes and setbacks occur; expectations are met and are not met.

The measures are a little more difficult for those whose changes cannot be fixed by making difficult but manageable cuts. You may need to make systemic changes; you may need to sell your home and relocate to a less costly location; you may need to contact your creditors to clarify the situation, asking that they cooperate with you while trying to resolve your current issue.

In any case, know your desired result, file your taxes, interact with creditors, monitor your progress, make decisions based on fair expectations, and work hard to move forward one step at a time. Every inch forward is a step in the right direction.

## Knowing About The Bare Bones Budget

Have you run out of money as a result of a drastic shift in your finances? Or maybe you're just thinking about how much you could be planning in case of an emergency in the future. In either case, a shoestring budget might be the answer.

1. What Does Bare-Bones Budget Mean?

A bare-bones budget is one that only includes the most important expenditures.

It satisfies all of your requirements but none of your desires. It's essentially a survival budget. It is the bare minimum needed to cover your living expenses

There are many reasons why you would want to make a bare-bones budget.

- First and foremost, if you find yourself in an emergency situation, you will have a guide to get you to navigate it. Knowing your bare minimum expenditures will assist you in rapidly identifying places where you can slash costs in the event of a crisis.
- Second, it's a perfect way to learn how much money you'll need to live. Understanding your needs will assist you in focusing on your goals and adapting your spending habits.
- Third, sticking to a strict budget is an excellent way to make significant progress toward a financial target. Using a bare-bones budget in the short term will help you meet your goals

quicker, whether you're paying off debt or creating an emergency fund.

2. **What Is Included In It?**

- A bare-bones budget should only contain the utter necessities for survival.
- Food, utilities, shelter, and transportation are what Dave Ramsey refers to as your Four Walls.
- For the majority of us, these fields include:
- housing services gas for vital transportation debt minimums essential food products basic phone service
- Another thing to double-check is the insurance coverage. Canceling your healthcare, house, and auto insurance can do more harm than good to your finances.

**What Isn't Here?**

We all have different facets of our lives that we believe are important enough to spend money on.

Suppose, you're trying to justify the expenditures mentioned below. In that case, you're probably not being honest with yourself about what constitutes a want versus a need.

Some of the following common expenditures should not be included in your bare-bones budget:

- Spending on entertainment cable or satellite apparel (unless required for work purposes)
- Restaurants, holidays, and hobbies will all benefit from massive data plans for your mobile phone.
- Personal treatment that isn't absolutely essential (hair coloring, manicures, cosmetics, etc.).
- It's easy to forget some of our usual spending patterns when creating a daily budget, but you must be brutally realistic about your needs when creating your bare-bones budget.

## Step By Step Guide To A Bare Bones Budget

Since the need for prioritization is mostly taken care of for you, creating a bare-bones budget is a little simpler than your usual budget.

Here's a step-by-step tutorial for creating a bare-bones budget.

**Step 1: Make a list of your expenses.**

Begin by listing all of your outflows from the previous month's expenses. Make a note next to obvious expenditures you'll want to carry over, such as your housing and utility costs, as you write stuff down.

**Step 2: Reduce Non-Necessary Expenses**

Start ticking off the expenditures on your list that aren't absolutely necessary. Anything that does not specifically affect your ability to survive should be eliminated.

**Step 3: Determine Your Necessities.**

Now that your expenses have been reduced, it is time to prioritize them.

You should prioritize the expenditures that are absolutely necessary for survival and have the least amount of wiggle room. You may negotiate some of your bills, but you need food to feed your family.

**Step 4: Reassess priorities and make further cuts.**

Consider this an exercise of self-assuredness.

Examine the spending for costs that you cannot remove but can reduce. For example, while your bare-bones budget will necessitate a phone for communication, an unlimited data plan will be a desire rather than a need.

**Step 5: Compile All of Your Remaining Expenses**

It's time to add them all up after you've listed, minimized, and prioritized until you've hit your bare minimums. Add it up to see how much money you need to make or have

1. **Why Would You Need A Bare Bones Budget?**

There are many reasons why you would need a shoestring budget.

A job loss or a medical emergency, for example, can cause you to change your spending. However, there are several other explanations why you would want to follow a more stringent budget.

Here are some common reasons why you would need to stick to a shoestring budget:

- Having to deal with a family crisis
- enduring a natural disaster.

Aa medical emergency or a sudden work loss

- debt repayment.
- Establishing an emergency fund.
- Breaking bad spending habits.
- Escaping the paycheck-to-paycheck loop.

A bare-bones budget is a valuable resource to help you get through difficult times, whether they need to stem from external influences or internal motives.

## 2. How To Make The Most Of Your Budget

Once you've produced your bare-bones budget, it's time to decide how and when you'll use it. As a guide, use your bare-bones budget.

Using your bare-bones budget as a roadmap to limit your expenses is an excellent way to make real progress toward your financial goals. A bare-bones budget will help you free up cash from non-essential expenses to put toward your goals, whether you want to pay down debt or build up your savings.

Make Your Budget Based on Your Bare-Bones Budget In the event of an emergency, such as a job loss, you would most likely need to replace your regular budget with your survival budget. Avoiding unnecessary costs in an emergency is critical to your financial well-being.

### 3. How Long Can Survive On This Budget?

The length of time you stay on a shoestring budget is solely dependent on your motivation. If an emergency has forced you to live on a shoestring budget, you can stick to it as long as your condition is unclear.

- You may pick your endpoint to correspond with meeting your goal or a specific milestone for more goal-oriented purposes.
- You might, for example, use a bare-bones budget before you can completely finance your emergency fund.
- Another choice is to use a bare-bones budget regularly and make financial sprints against your goals.
- This sprint strategy can be useful for achieving large objectives, such as paying off a large amount of debt.

- Maintaining a bare-bones budget for a long period can be difficult, but you should be able to motivate yourself to do so for at least a month.
- Monthly competitions are an excellent way to stay inspired and on goal.

Even if you just stick to a bare-bones budget for a month, you can see immediate savings. However, it can also assist you in identifying and eliminating long-term expenditures that will help you work your way to financial independence.

### 4. Some Tips For Setting Your Budget

On the surface, a bare-bones budget seems simple and straightforward, but in reality, it takes a lot of work to control your impulses. We're all used to living a certain way and spending in accordance with that way of life. It's not easy to give up anything like that.

Here are some pointers to help you survive on a shoestring budget.

#### a) Be Truthful About Yourself

The most important thing to consider when making a bare-bones budget is, to be honest with yourself. The aim of this budget is to save as much money as possible. If you try to persuade yourself that your Netflix, Spotify, and HBO subscriptions are essential for your well-being, you will fail.

You could have expenditures that others do not consider appropriate. You simply need to be frank with yourself about them. Daycare, for example, will be a necessary cost for a single mother who has to work. However, it will not be suitable for a stay-at-home mother in need of a few hours alone.

### b) Prepare for Unanticipated Expenses

As in every budget, it is important to account for the unexpected. There can be unanticipated necessities that arise, catching you off guard. Medication refills and medical appointments are easy to overlook and can throw your budget off track. Avoid this by budgeting for at least a small amount of unknowns in the future.

### c) Spend Less on the Essentials

Just because expenditure is necessary does not imply that you must pay the full cost for it. When it comes to saving money on needs, the first place to look is at food prices. Combine discounts, deals, and cash-back applications to save the most money at the grocery store. Check with your local grocery store to see if they receive fuel rewards for gift card purchases. You could save even more money by purchasing a gift card to pay for your groceries and receiving a discount on future gas purchases.

Find novel ways to enjoy the same activities without spending money.

You don't have to sit around and be bored just because you aren't spending money on movies.

There are many ways to have some fun that will not cost you a dime. Instead of going out, check your local paper and library for free activities, or try having friends over.

If you're used to eating out often, the suddenness of having to prepare all of your meals can be daunting. Make it easier by enlisting the help of friends and family. Throw batch cooking parties or take on pantry challenges with your mates.

A little bit of imagination can have a huge effect on your motivation and performance.

When you are tempted by a non-essential expense, use your imagination or search Pinterest or Google for ideas to achieve the same result without the cost.

### d) Concentrate on the Positive

Adopting a bare-bones budget can feel like a punishment, particularly if it results from an unexpected emergency, but it is critical to look on the bright side.

## CHAPTER FOUR

# Developing Your Budget Plan And Saving Money For The Plan

Your budget will be as unique as you are, or it won't work for you. Now that you know where your finances stand and have set dear goals, you're ready to take all of that information and create your money plan. The type of plan you build will depend on your most pressing priorities and goals, along with your earning, saving, and spending patterns. Taking all of these factors into account will help you create a plan you can truly live with instead of a budget that leaves you feeling frustrated, a budget that you'll probably ditch before long.

## Assessing Your Money Personality

Your budget really starts with you: how you handle money now and whether you'd like to change your relationship with money. If you know your money personality, you can frame your budget accordingly.

## Emotional spenders

Emotional spenders Buy more when they're angry, sad, or happy, leading to impulse purchases and credit card debt that derail other budget goals.

Creating spending blockades can help slow things down when the urge to shop strikes. Adding a special savings account to cover occasional overspending will help prevent excessive credit card debt.

## Status spenders

Status spenders Live large, buying big-ticket items, and keeping up with the latest everything. They're comfortable with risk (including risky investing) and debt, leading to budget breakdowns.

By budgeting for those big purchases and occasional losses, they can smooth out financial ups and downs and avoid running up unmanageable debt.

## Dodgers

Dodgers Avoid money stress by hiding from it (such as ignoring bills they can't pay). They don't think about or plan for the financial future, so they are often significantly behind on savings goals. Automating budget features (such as bill paying, expense tracking, and saving) reduces that stress and helps make sure nothing gets skipped.

## Mega savers

Mega savers Tend to be future-focused and risk-averse, prioritizing financial security over everything else. They avoid debt and invest ultra-conservatively, but those choices can also take a financial toll in the form of low credit scores and savings that don't keep up with inflation. The budget can address this by adding back these riskier categories in a secure way.

No matter which money personality best fits your situation, your budget can bring better financial balance and reduce financial stress.

# Simple Budgeting Strategies

## 1. The Simple 50-30-20 Method

For people who like to keep things super simple, a bucket budget does the trick. This classic 50-30-20 budget keeps things at a big-picture level, so you don't have to get bogged down in details. It's a perfect starter budget and one you can use as you're figuring out your financial priorities and goals.

**Here's how it works:**

- 5o% of your income goes into the needs bucket
- 3o% goes into the wants bucket
- 20% goes into the savings and investments bucket

Those percentages are not set in stone. For example, if your needs take up more than 5o percent of the money coming in, steal from your wants bucket (not your savings bucket). You can fiddle with the numbers until they make sense for your lifestyle.

## 2. The Debt Eraser

If your debt burden is crushing your finances, it's time to take charge. Setting debt paydown as your budget priority is the smart move here. This is where you'll see the biggest returns, more than even the most lucrative investments, especially if most of your debt comes from credit cards and another high-rate borrowing.

3. **The Wealth Builder**

This future-looking, no-more-worries budget focuses on creating and growing wealth. No matter how much money you have stashed away now, you can turn your budget into an amped-up savings plan. To achieve the overall goal here, you'll concentrate on adding income-producing assets to your net worth and minimizing spending on wants.

Once your needs are covered, your retirement and emergency savings are fully funded, and any debt payments are made, extra money in the budget goes toward buying assets. Income-producing assets include investments (such as stocks, bonds, and exchange-traded funds), rental real estate, and businesses. As these assets begin to produce income for you, you'll be able to increase your net worth even further.

### 4. The Room-For-Fun

If experiencing life is your top priority, you need plenty of room for fun in your budget—but that won't come at the expense of building up savings and paying down debt. This "here and now" budget carves out plenty of cash for the things you want to do: travel, scuba dive, host lavish dinner parties, whatever makes your life worth living. You'll still direct money toward savings (especially retirement savings) and debt payments, but any extra money in your budget goes into you "enjoy my life" fund.

To make this style work, you will have to make some trade-offs. You'll have fewer savings, and it will take longer (and cost more) to pay off your debt. Look for other places in your budget to slash costs, like downsizing your housing expenses or putting a hard freeze on buying stuff you don't absolutely need.

You can also find ways to turn your experiences into cash, like selling photos taken on your rain forest trek or writing golf course reviews (you'll find more details about this in Chapter 5).

### 5. The Unsteady Income

If you rely on side gigs or freelance income, budgeting presents some extra challenges. It's harder to plan when you're not sure how much money you'll have coming in next month, so this budget focuses on necessary expenses first and follows up with income from there. The trick here is to create a steady minimum income—sort of like a paycheck to yourself—that covers all of your absolute needs (including savings and debt payments), then comes back around a second time to cover the rest (like extra debt payments, money toward savings goals, and fun money) with "surplus" income. It can take a few months for this budget to really kick in, but once it does, you'll never worry about coming up short.

You need to know your income highs and lows over the last couple of years for this to work. Look back over your records, and figure out both the least and most money you received in a month. (This is the money you actually got, not the amount you billed or expected.) For budgeting purposes, the lowest monthly income amount is the one to use when you're working to figure out those first-pass expenses. Since, you'll probably bring in more than that most months, doing it this way builds in an automatic safety net. The "extra" money you bring in will go toward building a cash cushion.

When that cash cushion grows big enough to cover at least a full month's budget, you'll use it to create a steady "paycheck" for yourself, using previous income to cover this month's expenses. Whenever you get paid now, the money will go into the cushion account to pay next month's bills. Any time you have a surplus, funnel the extra cash into your highest-priority financial goal.

## Exploring The Envelope System

This expense tracking method is set up as a "cash in-person payment" method. You can automatically type things like retirement, mortgage, and some utilities. You can send checks or make a debit card payment online for other bills. But the expenses you pay in person only turn into cash.

At the beginning of the month, put cash in envelopes labeled with budget lines. Grocery shopping, entertainment, and restaurants are three great examples. Take your "grocery" envelope with you when you go to the store. Your spending comes to a halt when the envelope is empty. Your money follows; Paying cash can sometimes be inconvenient. Who wants to go to the gas station to pay in advance at the cash register? Who likes to count or follow the rhythm of the pieces? Also, with the rise of e-commerce, paying with cash is not always an option. Still, it's a powerful way to keep track of expenses because physically watching the money come out of the envelope inspires a whole new level of responsibility. To implement the envelope system, follow these steps:

1. **Check your budget**

The first thing needed is to know is how much money you are making and how much you are spending. In other words, you need to prepare a detailed budget for these items. The only way to know how much you plan to earn and spend each month

2. **Divide your expenses into categories**

Go over your budget and break it down into spending areas or categories you can pay for with a cash or debit card.

But there are other categories in which the envelope system can greatly help us control expenses and save money. For example, groceries, restaurant meals, personal expenses like haircuts and manicures.

Express the accounts once you've calculated how much money to spend, you need to do the math. How much money did you calculate to spend every fortnight or every week in these categories? Go to the bank on payday and get enough money to cover these expenses only.

If you are paid weekly, make a weekly withdrawal. If you get paid biweekly, make a biweekly withdrawal. And if you get paid monthly, make a monthly withdrawal to cover those expenses.

3. **Label your envelopes**

Obtain several envelopes and label each one with the expense

- Item.
- For instance:
- Supermarket
- Restaurants
- Entertainment

- Personal expenses

Several envelopes with you unless you also fill up the tank. When you need to pay, get enough money out of the correct envelope.

Before you go shopping, check how much is left in the envelope. If you arrive with the cashier, and it turns out that the account is $ 70 and you only have $ 60; you will have to leave something.

4. **IF YOUR MONEY runs out ...**

When the money in each envelope runs out, it's a sign that you've finished spending too. Avoid "borrowing" from an envelope to pay for expenses in another category. It would defeat the purpose of the envelope system. The goal is to get you used to budget, plan your purchases, and measure or limit your expenses.

If the money runs out in an envelope and you still have several days until the next fortnight, you will have to manage not to spend more. Another option is to review your budget and cut expenses from another category to fill the empty envelope.

Whatever the solution, don't overspend!

### Write the position on the envelope and save your receipt

Whenever you make a purchase, immediately write down the expenses and the corresponding envelope item. Also, take advantage of it and keep your receipt in the envelope. This way, you will keep an organized record. When you get home, write down the amount spent in your monthly budget.

### 5. Computer Spreadsheets

Many people are fans of spreadsheets and will tell you about their benefits until the end of time. The sheer number of templates, the ability to customize your budget, the beauty of having math for you on the screen are just a few of the benefits of spreadsheet budgeting.

### 6. Distribute the money among your envelopes

Divide the money you have withdrawn from the bank and put the corresponding amount in each envelope. Let's say you plan to spend $ 500 on food each month.

First, check your calendar and see how many weeks there are this month. Most have four weeks, but several months of the year have five.

Then divide the amount allocated to that category by the number of weeks. If that month has four weeks, then you would have $ 125 to spend each week. If the month is five weeks, you will only have $ 100 to spend on food each week

### 7. Use the money for what it is destined

Be sure to pay for all expenses in this category only with money from the envelope. If you go to the supermarket, do not take the gas. The two things to keep at the back of your mind with a budgeting app come from a single keyword: consistency.

Regardless of the method, you need to make tracking your spending into a habit to earn money. If you don't watch where your money is going, you are always wondering where it went. But when you set up with the right tools and know the work is worth it (which we verify from personal experience), you will go beyond good intentions to financial victories.

# Exploring The 50-30-20 System

You, like many others, may cringe at the word limit. That's understandable. For several years, budgeting has been portrayed as a difficult challenge. Nothing could be further from the facts. A budget is simply a plan for how you will spend your money. There are many budgets available that can meet various needs and lifestyles, and they don't have to be complicated.

If you want to simplify your budgeting process or if you're new to budgeting, the 50-30-20 budget may be a good fit. It consists of three simple measures that will assist you in prioritizing your monthly financial obligations. This budgeting form, also known as the **50-30-20 law**, is systematic and covers all the bases. Even suppose you don't want to do the math. In that case, there are several calculators available that can assist you with this process.

In this section, we will look at the 50-30-20 budget. It is how it operates and a nice 50-30-20 budget calculator that you can use right away.

Are you ready? Let's get started right away!

### 1. What is a 50-30-20 budget?

In its most basic form, the 50-30-20 budget law splits your after-tax profits into three distinct buckets. These are the buckets:

- 50 percent to requirements.
- 30% to desires.
- Savings of 20%

This strategy keeps your finances straightforward and easy to manage. This is an affiliate connection with a company we believe in. We could receive a commission that will help us expand. More details can be found in our disclosures.

### 2. How did the 50-30-20 budget come to be?

Elizabeth Warren, a United States Senator, devised the 50-30-20 budget. Senator Warren outlined this straightforward budgeting method in her book All Your Worth: The Ultimate Lifetime Money Plan. Not unexpectedly, it has stuck. People love how easy it is to understand and obey!

### 3. Why does the 50-30-20 rule work?

You may be wondering why this budget works. There are a few explanations for this. First and foremost, the budget is extremely basic. If you're not into specifics or are just starting out, this budget is fail-safe and simple to execute. It only focuses on three buckets - needs, wants, and savings - and fairly simple to understand. You don't have to waste time categorizing your finances.

Second, it allows you to keep track of every dollar you spend. You begin with your after-tax income, which represents 100 percent of what you have to work with, and then divide it into the various categories from there.

Finally, it can help you plan for big expenditures such as a house or vehicle, or it can help you pay off debt.

### 4. How to Make a Budget Using the 50-30-20 Rule

The 50-30-20 budget rule is very clear. To begin, calculate your after-tax income. After-tax income is essentially the sum of money left over after taxes are deducted. These taxes include federal, state, Medicare, and social security. Simply looking at your pay stubs is a fast and simple way to determine your take-home pay.

If, on the other hand, you own your own company, you can always measure your after-tax income. Subtract your gross revenue from your company expenditures and any state and federal taxes.

The fun starts after you've calculated your after-tax income. You can now divide your salary into three groups.

1. **Category 1: 50% Needs**

The first group is for all of your basic needs. This involves things that you absolutely cannot do without. You may provide rent or mortgage payments, health care, food, car payments, electricity, and debt payments. As you can see, the needs just involve things you need to live. This category does not include entertainment, take-out, or fine dining.

You should be able to satisfy your needs comfortably with half of your after-tax profits. If you are spending more than this, you may want to reconsider. Are you paying too much rent? Are you wasting more money on transportation than you can afford? Do you spend a lot of money on weekday lunches? In any case, you should make immediate adjustments to your expenses to reduce costs. To save money, you can either transfer to a more affordable home or start using public transportation. You can also make lunch at home and carry it to work.

2. **Category 2: 30% Wants**

Wants are any of the "good to have" that you spend money on. These are things you do not need in any way. Wants include going to the movies, dining out, new electronic devices, new handbags and shoes, and tickets to a big game. There are several suitable low-cost substitutes for wants. For example, you may want to purchase the most recent iPhone, but you can get the same benefits by purchasing an older model. You may want to join a gym, but you could also work out at home.

Almost anything you want to buy has a cheaper option. It is important to strike a balance between your wants and needs to enjoy some of these activities on occasion. However, exercise caution and common sense. The group of desires is the most difficult to master.

Some people's wants may involve high-end experiences that are financially out of control. For, e.g., someone will desire a new BMW when a Toyota would suffice. Use caution when it comes to your needs, as it can be easy to justify spending if you really want something.

### 3. Savings of up to 20% in Category 3

Savings is arguably the most critical category for your future. Savings in this context refers to both savings and investments. Savings can take several forms, from an emergency fund to a savings account. They can also include any money market investments you have.

Investments are any funds you have set aside to produce revenue. This may include investing in the stock market, buying real estate, or establishing retirement accounts. In this category, your emergency fund should be your highest priority. It is important to have three to six months' worth of living expenses invested in your emergency fund. Aside from that, prioritize your retirement savings. This may involve contributing to a company-sponsored 401(K) plan or an IRA. You might consider collaborating with an advisor to set this up.

Finally, debt repayment is a form of savings. You might be wondering how given that we had included debt payment in the "requires" category. Any purchases you make to cover the bare necessities fall into the "needs" category.

Additional contributions against interest and principal are called investments. This is because they are "saving you" from potential interest payments.

4. **Using a 50-30-20 budget calculator**

Creating your 50-30-20 budget does not have to be complicated. In reality, it can be as simple as using a simple budget calculator. Here's a 50-30-20 budget calculator created by Banzai in collaboration with Shinhan Bank. All you have to do is enter your post-tax salary, and it does the rest! You'll be able to quickly see how much to assign to each of the three groups.

## Exploring The Zero-Based Budgeting System

One of the easiest ways to improve your financial ability is to put your money to work. If you earn six figures a year or the minimum wage, every dollar you carry in is an opportunity to earn more. However, carefully allocating your finances entails more than just directing funds to your savings accounts. It's also the perfect way to prepare and save for the things that matter most to you, such as a trip to Bali or a down payment on a new home.

One of the most common methods is zero-based budgeting. Continue reading to see if this approach is right for you.

1. **What exactly is zero-based budgeting?**

Zero-based budgeting, also known as zero-sum budgeting, is based on the idea that each dollar in your budget should be classified. A zero-based budgeting scheme would tell you where 100% of your money went at the end of the month.

The distinction between a conventional budget and a zero-based budget is that a traditional budget allows excess money to accumulate in your bank account. A zero-based budget will force you to redirect the excess funds to investments, debt repayment, or another target. If you value productivity, reliability, and structure, this system might be just what you're looking for.

For the past seven years, money coach Nick True of Mapped Out Money and his wife Hanna have used a zero-based budget. Using this budget has compelled them to invest their money to more closely represent their objectives.

"A zero-based budget has helped us be more competitive with our money and invest it consciously in ways that resonate with our values," he said.

## 2. How to Make a Budget Based on Zero

Begin by making a list of all the areas where you spend money each month. This may include:

- Transportation and Housing
- Student loans, credit cards, and personal loans are all examples of debt.
- Financial savings
- Provisions
- Utilities and internet access
- Medical costs and health benefits
- Babysitting
- Have some fun!
- Memberships and subscriptions
- Personal hygiene
- Animals

- Donations and charitable contributions

Then, determine how much money you want to put together for each group. Estimate a fair number using your monthly credit card and bank statements. The fact that you use last month's income to decide how much you can spend is one aspect of zero-based budgeting. This way, you're just using money that's already in your bank account rather than counting on a potential paycheck. As a result, zero-based budgeting is particularly beneficial for consumers with variable income. After you've written it down, deduct your expenditures from your profits. If your expenses surpass your revenue, you will need to update your budget to save money.

If you have some money left over, you must categorize it. If you don't, you're more likely to spend it on something non-essential than on a long-term target. This is what zero-based budgeting is all about.

### 3. How to Put a Zero-Based Budget in Place

Following the creation of a budget, you must begin recording and categorizing your expenses. It's best to do this every day, or at least once a week, because waiting any longer can be daunting. Find a routine and a schedule that you can adhere to.

If you find yourself overspending in a particular category, take a step back and consider whether you need to raise the amount in that category – or find ways to eliminate the temptation.

You should also keep in mind that a zero-based budget is not static and should be changed as required. If Christmas is approaching, for example, you may want to spend more money on presents.

4. **How Does It Contrast with Other Budgeting Methods?**

A zero-based budgeting method necessitates more upkeep and vigilance than other types of budgets. Since you must assign a purpose to each dollar, you must also keep track of every dollar spent. This can be both time-consuming and aggravating.

If an unforeseen cost occurs in a zero-based budget, you must update your budget or use your savings.

True explained, "For example, I recently had to take my cat to the vet, and the bill was more than I currently had sitting in my pets category." “So I transferred funds from the clothes and dining out categories to the pets category to cover it for the month.” Since each transaction must be classified, zero-based budgeting requires you to confront how much you actually spend. Your budget will warn you if you continue to overspend on take-out or spontaneous Amazon transactions. A zero-based budgeting scheme cannot conceal spending habits.

5. **Some Budgeting Methods**

If a zero-based budget sounds too complicated or impossible to implement, consider the following alternatives: Budget of 50/30/20

Senator Elizabeth Warren's 50/30/20 budgeting approach is a basic budgeting scheme that works well for beginners.

The approach entails splitting your monthly income into three categories: 50% for needs, 30% for wants, and 20% for savings/debt repayment. When you make a purchase, you will categorize the item as a need, a want, or a savings/debt payoff.

Since there are so few categories, the 50/30/20 structure is simple to use and allows for personalization and improvisation.

It's a good option for someone who needs to budget regularly but considers zero-based budgeting too complicated or restrictive.

**Envelope Cash Method**

The cash envelope scheme entails paying for all qualifying expenditures with physical cash. You determine how much money to invest, withdraw it from your bank account, and divide it into envelopes labeled with the unit name. For, e.g., if you've set aside $500 for groceries, you'd withdraw $500 in cash and place it in an envelope labeled "groceries." The $500 should see you through the rest of the month. If you spend it by the end of the month and still need food, you'll have to take money from other categories, dig into your savings, or find some way to raise money.

This method is ideal for those who prefer a more traditional approach or those who need a little extra assistance in avoiding overspending in certain categories.

# CHAPTER FIVE

# Different Tools To Track Your Budget

There are several ways through which you can track your budget. You can use the old-fashioned ways of using a pen and paper or modern software and apps; the decision is yours. This chapter will walk you through some of the most common efficient ways to know about.

## Creating A Worksheet

No matter where you decide to house your budget, you'll need to start collecting information. To create a budget that you can live with, you'll need to know how much money you have coming in and going out and where that money usually goes.

If you prefer to go low-tech, you can work out your budget with pen and paper. With data breaches being reported with alarming frequency and the prospect of ransomware locking up laptops, many people are going back to basics when budgeting. This method gives you the most control over how you split out expenses, always includes things in the right categories, and doesn't come with recommendations, alerts, or "advice" that may sometimes feel condescending. Best of all, you will be intimately familiar with your finances, and that's a great way to build financial confidence for a more prosperous future.

1. **Setting Up Your Work She**

Suppose you keep track of your income and expenditures in a notebook or throw receipts and check stubs in a shoebox. In that case, you'll need a way to compile all of the data each month to get a full financial image. Accounting ledger paper is ideal for this; that is what the expansive sheets were intended for in the first place. Ledger paper is conveniently available online or at an office supplies shop. It comes in a range of sizes depending on the number of columns you need, so choose the size corresponding to the number of categories you're monitoring.

This traditional accounting tool allows you to record the specifics of each transaction, including the date, summary, dollar amount, category, and any other information you want to keep track of. If you choose to monitor by month, you can arrange each ledger sheet to carry an entire month's income and expense details by sorting your transactions using separate columns for different categories. If you prefer to monitor by group, create a separate sheet for each one, followed by a master sheet that consolidates all. If you have the time, you can record every transaction as it happens, ensuring that your data is still up to date. Otherwise, sit down with your records and an extra-large latte (or a beer, a bottle of wine, whatever makes you happy) regularly (at least once a month) and record them all at once.

### 2. Using Pre-Set Forms

Most office supply stores have budget forms you can use to track your income and expenses manually. Some even come printed on expense envelopes, making it even easier to organize receipts and keep tabs on your spending.

Tracking is harder using this method, making it difficult to see overspending until after the fact. If you want to go fully low-tech, you'll have to find a way (such as the envelope method) to stay on top of your daily spending to make sure you're staying within your budget limits.

### 3. Taking Care Of Your Credit Card Statement

When you're working your budget manually, dealing with credit cards calls for double duty. In addition to tracking payments made for each card and its running balance, you'll need to make sure you've accounted for all individual charges in their proper budget categories.

Along with the regular expense-recording worksheet you set up, it's helpful to create a separate sheet for each active credit card, meaning anyone card currently

in use or with an outstanding balance. The individual card worksheets will contain only high-level information for each month, which you'll pull from the statement. Record these five data points, each in a separate column:

- Total new charges.
- Total payments.

- Interest charges.
- Any fees (like for late payments).
- New statement balance.

With that data all in one place (instead of spreading out over a dozen credit card bills), you'll get a different perspective on your credit card situation. You'll notice different spending and payment patterns and see the direction your balance moves from month to month. These new insights will give you a bird's-eye view of your credit card usage and help you set better credit card—related SMART goals to get or keep debt under control.

## The Classic Envelope System

This time-honored budgeting method employs cash-filled envelopes to help you keep track of your monthly expenses. It's a perfect way to get used to budgeting because paying cash has a completely different impact than using a credit card and makes you more mindful of your spending. This allows you to feel more connected to your budget because your finances seem more genuine.

On the practical side, you create an envelope for each spending category in your budgets, such as rent, groceries, utilities, clothes, and gas. Then, each pay cycle, you cash your paycheck and divide it among the envelopes according to your budget categories.

If any of your envelopes has money left over at the end of the month, but the majority of it toward your top priority, and reward yourself for saving wisely with a (responsible) treat. Stop spending before the next pay period if you run out of money.

Here are some ground rules to follow:

I. When an envelope is empty, the category's spending for the month is complete. If you still need more, you'll have to take money from another group and change your budget in the future.
II. If you need to use a credit card to pay for something, immediately take the money from that category's envelope and place it in the credit card payment envelope.
III. When you do combo shopping (such as purchasing groceries and clothes at the same store), you can make money from different envelopes to keep your categories straight.
IV. If you have an envelope that you never (or rarely) use, exclude it from your budget.

V. You may also use a modified envelope scheme, in which you pay your daily bills with checks and use the cash envelopes only for everyday spending. Determine which method works best for sticking to your budget and stick with it.

## Creating A Budget Excel Sheet

If you like working with numbers and details, a spreadsheet budget may work well for you. Spreadsheets offer a lot of flexibility because you're the one setting up everything, so you can tailor your budget to suit your particular needs. You choose the categories and level of detail you want to track. You can set up visuals (like pie charts) or big-picture budget summaries to get an idea of where your finances stand at a glance.

These budget platforms require basic spreadsheet know-how plus regular time and attention to stay up to date. Plan to devote time every week for data entry. If you're great at gauging your spending, you can stretch data entry to a monthly chore.

The potential downside: you won't have real-time data (unless you update your worksheet every time you make a transaction), so you won't know how well (or poorly) you're following the budget after the fact.

While that won't affect your regular bills, it can leave you in the dark about daily spending. To make sure you don't go too far down an overspending rabbit hole, update your everyday spending at least weekly, even if you update everything else monthly.

### 1. How To Build A Budget Spread Sheet

Creating your budget spreadsheet is pretty straightforward. You can set up your worksheet any way you like, as long as it includes these five main columns:

- Description (of income or expense).
- Category (paycheck, housing, food, insurance, etc.).
- Budgeted Amount (what you plan to spend or receive).
- Actual Amount (what you actually spend or receive).
- Over/Under (the difference between the budgeted and actual amounts).

Once those are set up, you'll list all of your regular expenses and their categories (for example, electric bill/housing category) row by row. Those first two columns (Description and Category) will be the same every month, sort of like your own worksheet template.

Next, type in the monthly amount you expect to spend for each expense or receive income in the Budgeted Amount column. Enter income amounts as positive numbers, and expense amounts as negative numbers. The numbers can be locked into your template for fixed income and expenses, so you don't have to enter them repeatedly. For income and expenses that vary from month to month, your budgeted amount will be your target—what you expect to receive and the limit on how much you plan to spend.

2. **Built-In Templates**

Spreadsheet software typically comes with built-in family budget templates. All you have to do is enter your information, and the template does all of the calculations for you. These are really helpful if you're a spreadsheet novice or just don't have the time to start from scratch.

To set up the Over/Under column, you'll enter a simple formula for each line:

**Actual Amount- Budgeted Amount.**

Enter sum formulas at the bottom of each of the money columns to see your budget totals. If the total for the Budgeted Amount column comes out less than zero, you'll need to reduce some.

### 3. Using An Online Template

There are dozens of free budget templates available online, and they're all pretty similar. You can download many of the prefab templates right into Microsoft Excel, then customize them to fit your needs.

Kiplinger(www.kiplinger.com) has a good beginner household budget form that's straightforward and easy to use. You choose the budget period, then enter your categories (they list dozens of expenses that you can customize) and your budget target amounts in the online form. Once you've tailored the template to suit your needs, you can download the worksheet and open it in Excel. This is good for setting up your budget, but it doesn't offer any preset tracking capabilities.

Vertex42(www.vertex42.com) offers several different budget templates to choose from, and one is sure to fit your situation. You'll find worksheets for everyone from college students to families, covering various time frames (weekly, monthly, and annually). Its Money Management Template is set up to track spending and create reports (complete with graphs), so you can get a good handle on your budget.

You can also find a good basic budget form in the Toolbox on theConsumer.gov website (www.consumer.goy), courtesy of the Federal Trade Commission.

If you want to keep your budget housed online so you can access it from anywhere, try one of the money planner templates in Google Docs. You'll find a few different options in the Google Drive Template Gallery (www.docs.ggle.com/spreadsheets).

4. **Using Your Spreadsheet Correctly**

At the end of every month (or week or day), you'll gather all of your financial documents, such as bank statements, credit card statements, pay stubs, cash spending logs, and receipts. Then you'll enter your income and spending line by line in the Actual Amount column. Once you've typed in those numbers, your spreadsheet will automatically figure out the Over/Under for each line item.

When you're all done, check out the total in the Actual Amount column to make sure it's zero or positive, and check the line and column totals in the Over/Under

column to see how close you were to your expectations and whether you went over budget overall.

If your actual income and expenses match your projections well, you can leave them as is. If some of your line items are too far off for comfort, look at the reason for the mismatch. A one-time difference (such as a high electric bill during a heatwave) doesn't require a budget adjustment, but an ongoing underestimate (or overestimate) calls for a budget rewrite.

## A Bit Modern Budgeting Software

Budgeting software has been around for decades, and it's had plenty of time to work out all of the kinks. You'll spend a lot less time with setup than you would for a spreadsheet, but you may be more limited in your category and expense grouping options. Also, all of the budgeting software offers the option of linking your bank and credit card accounts so you can import information rather than having to type everything in yourself. Whether you prefer budgeting on your hard drive or in the cloud, there's a software solution for you.

**All** of the budgeting programs included here also offer apps so you can stay connected to your budget all the time.

1. **You Need a Budget (YNAB)**

"Give every dollar a job" is the first rule in the YNAB method. This program works on a principle called zero-sum budgeting, where every single dollar gets accounted for, zeroing out your budget every month. YNAB is a subscription service that works through your computer to help you get control of your money. The program links with your bank and credit card accounts to import transactions and offers an app that will sync up with your computer, so everything stays up to date. Focused solely on budgeting, YNAB doesn't bring in other aspects of personal financial planning

like investment tracking. You can try YNAB out for free for thirty-four days, and after that, it costs $83.99 a year ($6.99 a month, but you pay the full fee annually). You can learn more about this program at www.ynab.com.

## 2. Mvelopes

If you like the envelope method but not the idea of carrying all that cash around, look into Mvelopes. This software works the same basic way, offering digital envelopes for splitting up your money every month. It links to your bank and credit card accounts, lets you assign money to whatever envelopes you want, and lets you see what you've spent in the past. It also has an app that syncs up with your computer to manage your money on the go. Mvelopes has different subscription service levels, starting with the Basic version that costs $4 a month or $40 a year. You can take advantage of the thirty-day free trial at www.mvelopes.com to see if this budgeting method works for you.

## 3. Quicken

Quicken offers the soup-to-nuts version of personal finance software. The Quicken brand starts with a basic program and offers a ton of add-ons and upgrades as your needs get more sophisticated. Along with the budget building, transaction importing, and expense tracking, you can use the basic Quicken software to do things like manage your bills and track your spending.

The bare-bones version is Quicken Starter, which costs $34.99 a year. Quicken Deluxe adds in debt tracking and investment monitoring services for $49.99 a year. Quicken Premier offers even more tools, like personal financial forecasting, portfolio management, and even tax advice, for $74.99 a year. Both the Deluxe and Premier versions offer the first year for a discounted price. All versions of Quicken have to be installed on your computer to get you started. Quicken also offers a free mobile app that will sync up with the software. Find out which Quicken software might be right for you at www.quicken.com.

4. **Family Ties**

As of 2016, Quicken and TurboTax are no longer owned by the same company, but at tax time, you can still easily transfer your Quicken data right into TurboTax to make creating your return easier and less stressful.

## A Note: Always Keep Your Data Safe

Whether you're using a desktop or online software, it's critical to make sure your personal financial information is secure. These programs link to your bank and credit card accounts, and that means they have your passwords stored along with all the other sensitive information. Plus, software crashes and freezes can make your information inaccessible. So before you enter any information or set up links, take steps to protect your data.

- Make sure the data is encrypted and password protected.
- Run updated antivirus software on your computer.
- Never use public Wi-Fi to update personal financial software.
- Back up your data regularly (especially if you're not using online software).
- Use the most updated software version.

As long as you're vigilant with these strategies, your personal financial information should remain secure.

## Taking Your Budget On The Go With Apps

Suppose you want up-to-the-minute budget information 24/7 without the hassle of constant data input. In that case, budgeting apps will work best for you. Like software, these require a time investment for setup, including connecting your financial accounts and choosing your categories, but once that's done, the app will do all of the updating for you. Every transaction from your linked accounts will be automatically pulled into your budget in real-time, so there won't be any time lag when you're ready to check in all you'll have to do is look at your phone, and you'll know exactly where your monthly money stands.

1. **Just the Apps**

Both YNAB and Mvelopes offer app-only budget tracking if you don't want to deal with (or don't have) a computer, and the pricing is the same either way.

Budgeting apps usually also offer recommendations (like better deals on services you use), alerts (when you're nearing spending limits), and advice on how to manage your money (like when a credit card balance transfer might make sense).

What's more, all of the budgeting apps listed here are free (or at least have free versions), so you don't need to worry about spending money to save money.

### 2. Mint

Tried-and-true Mint was one of the first budgeting apps, and it still ranks high on the popularity list. This app comes with a wide range of features to tie your whole financial life together, but the budget component is the centerpiece.

Mint makes budgeting simple by pulling information from banks, brokerage firms, credit card companies, and other lenders so you'll have all of your information (from investment earnings to loan balances) in one place.

The app automatically tracks and categorizes your transactions in real-time, so you can tell in an instant whether you're sticking to your budget.

It offers up lists and colorful graphs so you can get the overview at a glance. You can even set up alerts to let you know if you are going over budget or running out of cash.

One downside: ads. For example, if you buy beach towels and sunscreen, Mint might serve you up an ad for sunglasses. If you hate having your screen cluttered up by these targeted ads, you might want to cross Mint off your list.

### 3. Wally Lite

If you want just a very basic budgeting app, check out Wally Lite. It keeps track of income and expenses as you go and serves up current budget snapshots to help keep you from going over. It even lets you take and save pictures of your receipts for your records, rather than having to enter expenses manually. It captures where you are (via location services) to automatically identify the type of purchase you're making for quicker categorizing, and the more you use it, the "smarter" it gets. The app also lets you set savings goals and track progress toward meeting them as part of your budget.

This app isn't as intuitive as some of the others and can be a little harder to navigate if you want to keep track of more than just your income and expenses. But if you mainly want to tap into its budgeting capabilities, it's very straightforward. On the downside, you can't access Wally through your computer, only through the app.

One unique special feature: Wally can handle foreign currencies (unlike most other budgeting apps), making a huge difference if you travel internationally or move out of the US.

4. **PocketGuard**

If you have trouble keeping your spending under control, the PocketGuard app may be able to help. Like other budgeting apps, PocketGuard links up with your accounts and compares your actual spending to your plan. You can set and track savings goals and set hard spending limits. It's also one of the easiest budgeting apps to set up, partly because it's budget-only focused and doesn't tie together your entire financial picture.

Along with its other features, PocketGuard actively looks for ways to save money on your regular bills (like phone or cable) by seeking out better deals. Plus, with its In My Pocket feature, you can see how much money you really have available to spend every day—not just the balance of your bank account. On the downside, PocketGuard doesn't track goals, like savings.

### 5. Simple

Simple takes a different approach by focusing on the banking side of budgeting. In fact, it essentially takes the place of a traditional checking account (complete with bill paying, a Visa debit card, and fee-free ATMs) with the added bonus of built-in budgeting. Anything you can do with a standard checking account, you can do here, like set up direct deposits, earn interest, and transfer money.

Simple tracks your spending on the budgeting side and lets you set up envelope-like spending goals, so you never go over budget. The app offers goal setting and tracking features, including a special spot for emergency savings. It also lets you know what's safe to spend based on what's really going on in your account (upcoming payments, for example) rather than just your available balance.

### 6. Goodbudget

If you're budgeting as part of a couple, the Goodbudget app can help. The Goodbudget system is based on the envelope method and lets you sync up two devices so you and your significant other will always be on the same financial page. This is a great way to track spending when you're not together so you can tell when an expense envelope is empty (or almost empty). The app also lets you split

transactions among multiple envelopes, which works great when you're shopping in stores where one trip may hit several spending categories.

### 7. Keep It Private

If you're nervous about putting so much private financial information in one place, look at the app's security measures before you choose it. The best security includes high-level encryption, multifactor authentication, and the ability to shut down mobile access to your account if your phone goes missing.

The free version of this app offers ten envelopes and maintains one year of history. The Goodbudget Plus version offers unlimited envelopes and accounts, five-device connectivity, access to five years' worth of budget history, and email support for $6 per month (or $50 per year).

## CHAPTER SIX

# Tracking And Analyzing Your Progress

If you want to win with cash, you have to exchange your actions with money. The way to do this is by budgeting and sticking to it. The way you do it is to keep track of your expenses. This might be new terminology for you, but don't be intimidated. We can give you the details you need to advance your money journey (with confidence!) While taking you away from what's holding you back.

## Keeping Track Of Your Budget

In order to track your Budget, you will need to follow following steps.

**Step 1: Make a budget.**

Without one, you won't be able to keep track of your expenses.

What is a budget? This is your monthly fundraising plan – your expected income and expenses are ranked for the entire month. A budget does not control you; you control it. It is a guide that you implement to make sure your money does what you tell it to do. There are three basic steps to budgeting:

- Write down your monthly income.
- Write down your monthly expenses.

Start with food, housing (your mortgage or rent plus utilities), clothing, and transportation. Once covered, list all other expenses such as entertainment, restaurant meals, pan flute lessons, TV streaming services, gym memberships, donations, savings, etc., budget percentages. Make sure your income minus your expenses is zero. If the math doesn't work, you need to adjust your categories until you get that zero-based budget.

**Step 2: Record your expenses**

Daily. We think so. All. Day. If you don't keep track of what you spend, you will be living in a great country where wallets are never empty and bank accounts are full and full. It would be cool, but it's not the real world. In the real world, you need to keep track of what you are spending. This action is essential to communicate to you and your spouse how much money is left to use in all the categories that you defined in the first step. And that brings us to the next step.

**Step 3: Check these amounts**

Tracking your expenses can help make sure you're not overspending in any one area. When entering an expense, be sure to keep track of how much is left in that category.

If you are married, be sure to record all expenses and register before spending. It is excellent for accountability and communication. That way, neither of them would say, "I didn't know they were spending most of their entertainment budget getting tickets to the wax museum. I wanted to sign up for a couples beatbox class. "Budgets inflate when you don't track and monitor your spending.

## Why Is It Important To Keep Track?

We just talked about it, but now we go further. Because let's be truthful, if all you do at the beginning of each month is write or write budget lines and assign totals to each item, you are not committing to stick to those lines.

Many of us have started "budgeting" in this way. And that's a start. It is good to have an idea of where the money should go. But if you don't keep track of your expenses, you don't know where your money is going. You risk continually setting unrealistic budgets and never reaching your wonderful financial goals, and that's not what we want for you. Remember: we want you to be successful! So let's take a look at the different methods to achieve it.

## Understanding The Process Of Budget Evaluation

However, these spreadsheet aficionados aren't necessarily married to other spreadsheet aficionados. Couples should discuss their expenses openly; don't let spreadsheets get in the way of your happiness for the rest of your lives.

The second disadvantage to spreadsheets is that you must use your machine to keep track of your expenditures. If you don't have time to enter expenditures on such regular trips, the budget isn't a budget; it's only a spreadsheet full of good intentions. Good intentions are a good place to start, but they will not get you far in life.

You probably think spreadsheets will be useful because you spend a lot of time on your computer. But do you know what's really there for you? It's your phone. This brings us to the next choice, which we confidently declare to be the BEST for keeping track of your spending. The Budget Evaluation is a series of review processes used to continuously assess the physical and financial advances achieved at any given time and their contrast with the Modified Institutional Budget (PIM) and their effect on achieving institutional objectives. Evaluating your budget is an important step in ensuring that it aligns with your current financial goals. Since your needs and priorities will change over time, you should review your budget regularly.

## Purposes of The Budget Evaluation

Determine the degree of "Efficiency" in the budget execution of income and expenses and compliance with the budgetary goals contemplated in the activities and projects for the period under evaluation. Determine the degree of "Efficiency" in fulfilling the budgetary goals about the budgetary execution of the expenses made during the period to be evaluated.

Explain the deviations presented in the behavior of the execution of income and expenses, comparing them with the estimate of financial resources and the forecast of expenses contemplated in the Institutional Opening Budget (PIA) as well as in the Modified Institutional Budget (PIM) and determine the causes that originated them.

Achieve a general analysis of the budget management of the specifications for the first semester of this year, linked to the production of goods and services provided to the community.

## The Steps To Evaluate A Budget

1. **Look at your current goals and objectives:**

First, you must ask yourself what your current goals are because these tend to change over time. You may have focused on getting out of debt, and once you meet that goal, you may have a lot of extra money to redistribute. Suppose you plan to get married soon or have a child. In that case, your financial situation will change dramatically, and you will need to work on a family budget.

2. **Review your current budget:**

Next, you should evaluate your current personal budget to see if it is on track to meet those financial goals and help. This can be pretty straightforward, but you will have to change your budget if something has changed recently. Look for ways you can improve it; for example, you may find that you need to put your savings in a different bank so that it is more difficult to access the money.

This can add additional incentives to keep track of your expenses throughout the month, cut down on some categories, or cut expenses that may now seem unnecessary.

3. **Change your budget:**

If tracking your spending is the only thing you hate about your budget, consider switching to an envelope system or switching to another savings method.

**Evaluate your new budget:** Lastly, evaluate your new budget at the end of the month. This will help you make sure that it works well for you and that the changes are working. You will need to make a few small changes to certain categories, but this process shouldn't take long.

## Some Hearty Tips

I. It can be beneficial to look at your annual budget as well. Take a look at spending patterns to see where your money is going. This can help you make changes and prioritize your spending so you can meet your financial goals.

II. Taking the time to evaluate your budget when setting your new goals or creating a financial plan can help you stay on track. Ensure you have a few splits planned as part of your budget; this can make it easier to stick with it.

III. You must also ensure that you remove something that isn't required. Look at the things you like best, prioritize them, and then cut out the ones that bring you the least satisfaction.

IV. It may take some time to notice this out and define your priorities, but doing so will help you get your budget work done.

V. Evaluating a budget is a simple process that will help you rethink your financial plan so that, over time, it adapts to your new needs, goals, and priorities to help you meet your goals in life.

## The Process Of Reviewing Your Budget

A personal budget is a wonderful tool due to its clarity and transparency. However, you must work with your budget to make it meaningful and to benefit from the value it can deliver. If you don't, your budget becomes nothing but a hollow shell.

A budget review needs to be performed when your initial budget is prepared and at least once every month after that. This review is based on the budget formula mentioned earlier:

(Total) Income — (Total) Savings — (Total) Expenses = Financial Health.

I added the words "total" to the formula because it would be too cumbersome, to sum up, all line items individually. Instead, it would be best to use the totals you have already compiled earlier for each of the budget components (income, savings, and expenses).

Once you reconcile these totals, your calculation will result in one of the following three possible outcomes, signaling the status, or health, of your financial situation:

1. **Healthy**

Your financial status is "healthy," which is indicated by a positive result of your budget formula. You are in the black, meaning that your income is covering your savings, as well as your expenses and still leaves you with a residual amount. A healthy financial status would allow you to save for emergencies, retirement, financial goals, pay for your monthly expenses and still have money left over to play with. This is the most desirable status we all like to be in.

2. **Balanced**

Your financial status is "balanced," indicated by the result of your budget formula. You break even, meaning that your income is covering your savings, as well as your expenses, although not leaving you with any residual amount. A balanced financial status would allow you to save for emergencies, retirement, financial goals, and pay for your monthly expenses. While you would not have any surplus money left over, this is still a totally good financial status.

### 3. Unhealthy

Your financial situation is "unhealthy," as shown by a negative budget formula outcome. You're in the red, which means your earnings aren't (fully) covering your savings and expenses. An unfavorable financial situation will prevent you from (fully) saving for emergencies, retirement, or other financial goals. It will also not be enough to cover (all of) your monthly expenses. It's even worse because you'd have to delete any of your current savings or go into debt to make up for the shortfall (which is your budget deficit). This is a dangerous financial situation that we do not want you to be in because it is completely unfair and unsustainable.

When researching the subject of budgeting, you will often come across writers who recommend that a budget be measured solely on income and expenditures, either by considering savings as a cost item or by accounting for savings at a later point in the budgeting process.

Savings, in my humble view, are not an expense. Savings are extremely important for your future. They deserve their own budget group to highlight their significance and ensure they are still top of mind. This understanding goes far beyond mere wordplay.

My more proactive approach considers your savings rate as the second most important factor, right after your salary. What is the reason for this? And suppose you do not prioritize your savings over your expenses. In that case, you will be tempted to compromise your savings rather than your expenses when you are in financial difficulty.

What I am advocating, on the other hand, is the polar opposite. If you find yourself in a bad financial situation, the first thing you can do is reevaluate and optimize your spending habits without affecting your savings.

Your investments are "holy" to you. Suppose you erode your savings repeatedly or over time. In that case, you risk not having enough funds when catastrophe hits (this relates to your emergency funds), your working life ends (this relates to your retirement funds), or you need money to achieve your financial goals.

So, what would you do if you're in debt? Let's take a closer look at your choices, shall we? First and foremost, if you are in a bad financial situation, do not panic. There are numerous options available to you to boost your financial situation (without having to borrow money):

I. **Revisit your expenses.**

Your single biggest lever is your expenses. But not all expenses are alike. You have expenses for essentials (so-called needs) and non-essentials (so-called wants). Essential expenses (needs) are required for your living and hard to modify or compromise on short-term.

Examples are your rent, health insurance, utilities (public/private)transportation to work, and taxes. Non-essential expenses (wants) are not necessarily required to survive and much easier to modify and compromise on short-term (as they represent lifestyle choices that can more easily be altered). Examples are your entertainment cost, restaurant visits, clothing, footwear, laundry cost, tobacco, and alcohol. Critically review and challenge your expenses for non-essentials (needs). Tighten your belt and stop frivolous spending. You will most certainly find expenses that you can reduce or eliminate, at least provisionally. You should do the same analysis with your essential expenses (needs), although with this expense type, a positive budget impact takes longer to become effective.

**II. Revisit your earnings.**

Typically, a thorough expense review yields enough saving opportunities. However, should this not be sufficient, you could seek possibilities to increase your income. Maybe you can find a higher-paid job or accept this promotion you have been offered (but so far rejected for whatever personal reason). Maybe you could work overtime, start a part-time job, or any other side hustle. As with essential expenses, it takes time before your budget benefits from such a move, as this option can typically not be implemented on short notice.

**III. Revisit savings for short-term goals.**

Finally, and only if the first two solutions are insufficient, you should consider how much you save each month for your short-term financial goals. These are the ones you would be able to postpone a little by spending less. Alternatively, you might consider putting these savings on hold for a few months. However, avoid touching your investments for mid-term and long-term goals because they usually provide more value to you than short-term goals. Compromise on these targets would cause much more pain and regret than deferring the accomplishment of your short-term goals. Under no circumstances, and I repeat, under no circumstances should you touch your retirement or emergency savings (unless a real emergency occurs, of course). As previously said, these savings are much too large for your financial wellbeing.

You now understand how to "spell your budget" and what to do if you find yourself in the red. After this heavyweight stuff, it becomes easier from here on out.

Using a budget is a critical foundation for managing the finances most efficiently and competently possible. Although we discuss a budget in a personal finance sense, the term "professional" is used on purpose.

It is important to use a dependable or professional budget to achieve financial freedom and independence.

Although the degree of formality and granularity can be debated, a budget is a "must-have" method. And with practice, it becomes easier. It will eventually become a habit in which you will no longer need to spend much time.

It will become ingrained in your mind. It will guide your financial decisions, and you will almost automatically find yourself in a balanced or stable financial situation with little, if any, need to induce corrective steps. There are a few other items to keep in mind for your budgeting routines:

**a) Frequency**

Get into the rhythm and perform your budget review at least monthly. Compare actuals with planned amounts and see if there is anything you can learn or must improve going forward.

**b) Discipline**

For your budget to work, you should update it regularly. While you can do the budget analysis monthly, you want to input your financials more often so that the monthly review does not take that long.

### c) Automation

Set up electronic payments to streamline the process. This will not only make recording and classification of your financial transactions more comfortable, but it will also prevent you from sabotaging your system (this way, you cannot tamper with savings, for example, as they are directly deposited into your respective bank accounts).

### d) Accountability

Whether things work out well or not, you are accountable. Don't blame anybody else. Master your own financial universe, and do not search for responsibility

elsewhere. Look into the mirror. If you do not like what you see, change it.

### e) Consistency

If something does not work according to your planned budget, make up for it in the next budget. Be consistent with your budgeting and stick to it.

Things will work out eventually. But it takes time and perseverance.

### f) Honesty

Don't cheat yourself. It makes no sense to overstate your income or understate your expenses. Get real, and do not jeopardize the meaningfulness of your budget.

### g) Budget changes

You might be asking, "Will my budget change over time?" In a word, yes. Perhaps your salary will increase, commensurate with your education and experience. Your expenses will undoubtedly change when you make serious investments, such as buying a new car or your first home.

Your budget may also change due to adverse circumstances, such as losing a job or an unexpected bill, such as a medical emergency. In a worst-case scenario, your emergency fund may be wiped out completely, and you may need to make drastic budget adjustments to refill the fund.

Suppose you have kept track of your income and expenses for a more extended period. In that case, you will notice that your budget keeps changing to mirror your current circumstances. This is nothing to be alarmed about in any way. That's normal. A budget can and must handle all sorts of changes. It is flexible and will, in any case, be reviewed and adjusted every month.

The best budget is worthless if you do not work with it consistently. Be disciplined and adhere to your budget as it relates to your saving and spending routines. Once a month, you need to review and analyze your budget to pinpoint your financial performance, learn from mistakes and make adjustments where needed. Your budget formula (Income — Savings — Expenses = Financial health) reveals if you have placed in a "healthy," "balanced," or "unhealthy" financial situation. If you are in the black, your income covers your savings and expenses, and you even have a residual cash amount to play with at your discretion. If you are in the red, challenge your expenses first, especially your non-essential spending. While it might be unavoidable, (long-term) savings are sacred and should not be slaughtered prematurely to compensate for short-term deficits.

# CHAPTER SEVEN

## How To Stick With Your Budget Plan

It is difficult to stick to a budget. You have a bad month, become disheartened, and give up. Or you believe you can keep your budget in your head, and that is sufficient. You could, and it could be, but this is not the case for most people.

### Strategies To Stick to Your Budget

The reality is that a budget will help you achieve your objectives. It's a tremendously useful tool that everyone can learn. For others, it simply has a steep learning curve.

We want to provide you with the tools, resources, and strategies you need to succeed. Kylaina Afonso, Assistant Branch Manager at Valley

First's Downtown Kelowna branch, shares 11 budgeting tips to help you get started, meet your goals, and succeed.

1. **Take your time while making large transactions.**

Take a week to think about it if it's not something you require. Is this purchase accompanied by a payment plan (e.g., a car loan) that will disrupt your budget? Will this deplete your savings? How can this help you in your daily life? Is the advantage worth the cost?

Weigh the benefits to ensure that it adds value to your life while not putting a strain on your budget. If you've forgotten about it after a week, that's a pretty good indication that you didn't really need it.

2. **Never spend more money than you have available.**

Getting into debt can be a vicious cycle that is difficult to break. You end up paying more in interest than you would have if you had waited or saved up. If you can't afford anything you want, postpone it for a week. Plan ahead of time if you intend to go on holiday. Save daily to keep your spending on track.

Eating Mr. Noodles for four months after a holiday is most likely not your definition of "living your best life."

3. **Maintain a lower credit card cap.**

Credit cards with high limits are easy to accumulate and difficult to pay off. Reduce your exposure to temptation! Maintain a lower credit limit and pay it off more often to avoid being stranded.

A simple rule of thumb is to stick to a maximum amount that you can pay off at once (e.g., using an emergency fund). As a result, you will pay for your purchases with little to no interest while still safely building your credit.

4. **Set the budget to zero.**

When you budget to zero, your revenue less your expenditures equals zero. Income minus expenses equal $0

When you budget to zero, you put every dollar you receive to work, whether it's savings or an additional loan payment. You do not provide yourself with a buffer or extra padding. This is a progressive approach to gaining full financial influence.

Budgeting to zero does not imply that you spend every penny you earn. It also does not imply that you must stick to your categories for the whole month. On the opposite, it is a perfect way to start a savings program by incorporating your savings into your budget and keeping your budget flexible enough to adjust to the curve balls that life throws at you.

5. **Take part in a no-spend challenge.**

This is also known as a spending freeze, spending easy, or a zero spends challenge. Whatever you name it, the concept is the same: a pledge not to waste money on something that isn't necessary. You can participate in a no-spend challenge for a week, a month, or even an entire year! It may seem extreme, but it is a surprisingly powerful way to shock your system, cull your spending habits, and transform your money attitude.

Begin your no-spend challenge by writing down what counts as a need and how long you want to go. Make it more interesting by challenging your best friends or family members to see who can save the most money.

6. **Keep it simple.**

Minimalism has become increasingly common in recent years. As a result, it has received both praise and criticism. However, apart from the hype, there is financial merit to it.

Here's how you can begin with minimalism: Determine your desires and needs. Reduce your desires and focus on your needs. This will immediately reduce the budget and make it much easier to stay on track. Is there a new pair of Nikes out now? It's a good thing your pair from last year is still in good condition. Saved $100!

Another approachable way to approach minimalism is to reduce clutter: do you even need a subscription to both Apple Music and Spotify? What about Netflix, Amazon Prime, Hulu, CraveTV, and cable, among others? Each of these services is just $10 a month.

Take a look at your banking to see if you can get rid of any fees. How much do you pay in monthly payments, and how much do you pay in transaction fees on top of that? Consider converting to a free account, such as our Simply Free Account, and you will save at least $179.40 per year (based on average monthly bank fees of $14.95 at major Canadian financial institutions).

7. **Make a meal plan**

Planning your meals and sticking to a shopping list are two of the simplest ways to save money. You won't overbuy foods that will go bad in your fridge (and then throw them away — a waste of food and money) if you prepare what you need for the week.

8. **Shop for groceries online.**

If you've ever gone grocery shopping on an empty stomach, you know that a lot of non-essentials creep into your cart. These small $2-$5 extras can often account for the bulk of your grocery bill. Or have you ever gone to the produce section and felt compelled to change your eating habits, throwing vegetables you couldn't even pronounce in your cart, just to have 75 percent of them sit in your fridge and go bad?

You can shop online and pick up or get your groceries shipped to you in Canada at the following grocery stores:

Supermarket Save On Foods IGA Walmart Thrifty Foods No Frills

Buying groceries online not only saves you time and eliminates impulse purchases. These websites also allow you to save your grocery list for future trips, which helps you keep your grocery budget consistent.

9. **Take care of yourself first.**

Set up some automatic transfers or put some money aside on payday to account for your payments, but most importantly, for YOU. Future-you would be really happy if you put money into your savings, TFSA, or RRSP every payday before you start spending your hard-earned money.

Also, small sums add up to greater sums, which can eventually be used to purchase a holiday or pay for an emergency engine repair on your vehicle. Or maybe it will help you one day buy a house?

In any case, by paying yourself first, you are ensuring that you place yourself in a position of importance and acknowledging that if anyone deserves your hard-earned money, it is you.

**10. Compare brand names**

Name labels cost Canadians an additional 8-9 percent more per shopping trip than generic brands. That may not appear to be a lot per object. However, it can add up throughout a single shopping trip. Consider how much money you spend on a brand name per year if you shop twice a month.

Is that Name Brand item really worth the extra money? It's often worth spending a little more for a high-quality item that you won't have to substitute as often. When you spend more, you want to make sure you're getting quality and not just investing in brand real estate.

Contrast the store brand with the name brand. What are the nutrients like in food, for example?

Are they essentially the same, with the same ingredients and daily intake values? If that's the case, what's the point of investing more money on practically the same thing?

**11. Tie your expenses to your job.**

You put in a lot of effort to earn your money. However, when people spend money, they seldom link it to the labor that went into making it. But you buy the $100 pair of shoes without giving it much thought.

However, if you consider how much labor those shoes will need, you can reconsider their worth. Here's how to go about it: Determine how much you are paying per hour. Divide your gross pay by 52 weeks, then by the number of hours you work in a week. when you're ready to buy something, calculate how many hours of labor it will need. So the shoes aren't cheap.

They take 3 hours and 38 minutes to complete. Thinking about your whole budget in this way is an easy way to mentally reframe your relationship with money.

# Some Budgeting Tips To Help you

Unfortunately, the term budget has a poor reputation. When it comes down to it, a budget is simply a plan for your money. Budgeting implies that you are investing with intention until the month starts. Unfortunately, many people regard a budget as a shackle that prevents them from doing what they want.

That, however, could not be further from the facts! A budget does not restrict your rights; rather, it grants you freedom! It all boils down to being deliberate about where your money goes.

**How Can Budgeting Assist Me?**

A budget will provide you with a course of action and a clear picture of where your money is going each month. Budgeting will help you reach your goals, whether they are to get out of debt, save for retirement, or just prevent your grocery bill from spiraling out of control.

When you view budgeting as simply saving your money purposefully, you will find that you have more freedom to spend! Once you've budgeted for something, you'll be able to spend it without feeling guilty. Many people claim to have "extra" money after creating and sticking to a reasonable budget. Isn't that incredible?

**1. Decrease the budget to zero before the start of the month.**

This means that you're making a schedule and assigning a name to each dollar before the month even begins. It's known as a zero-based budget. That doesn't mean you have no money in your bank account. It simply means that your profits less all of your expenditures equal zero.

**2. Work on the budget as a group.**

If you're married, have a family budgeting night once a month. Make it enjoyable! To help you concentrate, grab some of your favorite snacks and put on a good playlist.

You need to be on the same page regarding finances, so set goals together and fantasize about the future. Remember, if you and your partner are one, your bank accounts should be as well! It is no longer your or my money; it is our money.

if you're single, find someone to serve as your accountability partner and help you stick to your goals!

**3. Keep in mind that each month is special.**

Some months, you'll need to set aside money for items like back-to-school supplies or regular car maintenance. Other months, you'll be putting money together for vacations, birthdays, and holidays. Regardless of the occasion, make sure you budget for those expenses. Keep those special days from creeping up on you by pulling up your calendar when you're putting together your budget. (Hint: Christmas is back in December this year!)

As things change, make sure to adjust your budget each month. Create a savings account in which you can deposit money during the year. You will be stressed if you do not have a strategy. And it takes all of the joy out of giving and celebrating. That is not what everyone needs!

**4. Begin with the most critical categories.**

Giving and saving come first, followed by the Four Walls: food, services, shelter, and transportation. Once you've taken care of your true needs, you should fill up most of the budget categories.

**5. Clear your debts.**

If you have debt, paying it off should be your highest priority. To get out of debt as quickly as possible, use the debt snowball strategy and the 7 Baby Steps. Take it on! Become enraged! Stop allowing debt to rob you of the very thing that allows you to succeed financially—your profits.

**6. Don't be afraid to cut costs.**

Prepare yourself! It could be time to make some changes in your life. If money is tight right now, you can easily save money by canceling cable, eating out less, and shopping at discount clothes and grocery stores.

Keep in mind that the budget cuts are just temporary. You can still make changes later.

**7. Establish a timetable (and stick to it).**

When you're making a budget a regular part of your routine, why not set aside particular dates for other expenses? To pay your bills, you might set up auto drafts from your checking account. Alternatively, you might purchase your groceries regularly, such as once a week or twice a month. When you know what to expect and when to expect it, you eliminate many stress and possible problems.

**8. Keep track of your success.**

It's important to check in on your progress from time to time. If you're dating, keep track of your expenses and purchases together so you can both stay on track. Examine the previous budgets to see how far you've progressed. And don't forget to rejoice in the small victories.

**9. Set aside any money in your budget for a rainy day.**

Set aside a small sum of money for unforeseen expenditures during the month. In your budget, categorize this as miscellaneous. That way, if anything comes up, you can cover it without having to take money from anywhere else. Keep track of any expenditures that end up in this group regularly. You will eventually want to promote them to a permanent position in your budget.

**10. Discard your credit cards.**

If you're serious about sticking to a budget and getting out of debt, you'll have to give up your credit cards for good. From employing them! Cut them up, shred them, or use them in a craft project! Get them out of your life, whatever you have to do.

With no credit card debt, there will be no more minimum payments to add to the budget, no penalties or high-interest rates to deal with, and far less tension and worry.

Stick to debit cards (and even cash!) and toss those credit cards out the window like your ninth-grade fling. What's the best thing about using a debit card? The money is taken directly from your bank account! There is no middleman to charge you 15% interest.

**11. Use cash for budget categories that are causing you problems.**

If you are continually overspending on your food budget or on fun money, cash out those categories and use the envelope system to keep yourself accountable. Simply go to the bank and withdraw the amount of cash you've budgeted for that category. Avoid investing until the money runs out! It is the ultimate responsibility companion.

**12. Make use of an online budgeting tool.**

If pen and paper (or spreadsheets) aren't your things, it's time to embrace the digital age and use a budgeting tool like Every Dollar. You can prepare a budget and monitor your expenses from the convenience of your smartphone! You can also sync your budget with your partner, which helps keep the lines of communication open.

**13. Be happy and stop making comparisons.**

You have a lot more than you think. Don't equate the condition to that of others. Comparison will rob you not only of your joy but also of your paycheck. Continue to move forward and do what is best for your family.

**14. Set goals for yourself.**

Suppose you're paying off student loans, putting money together for an emergency, or paying off your mortgage. In that case, you need to remember why you're doing it. What motivates you to make these sacrifices?

**15. Show yourself a lot of grace.**

It normally takes three to four months to get a grip on the budgeting process. It will not be perfect the first or second time. But don't worry, you'll get there!

## Budgeting Tip for Unpredictable Income

Guys, I have good news for you!

You should budget if your income is unpredictable or erratic. A reasonable rule of thumb is to budget based on what a low-income month looks like for you. This will be your salary for budgeting purposes. This is how it works:

- Make a list of the things you'd include in your budget. Include things such as giving, saving, the Four Walls, and so on.
- Sort the list by priority. What would you do if we had a bad month and just had enough money to do one thing on this list? Put a 1 beside the thing.
- Continue your journey. List your second goal with a 2 and work your way through your budget, marking things in order of importance. Always remember the necessities come first.

This approach makes the budget work for you and shows you where your money is going.

**How To Develop A Budget Quickly**

If you're still in debt and haven't started saving for an emergency fund, you're in Baby Step 1. That means your aim for this stage of your financial journey should be to save, save, save! I've put together a budgeting guide just for you.

Wherever you are on your financial path, the easiest way to create a budget is to use Every Dollar, our free budgeting tool—you can plan out next month's budget in as little as 10 minutes! Using our premium edition inside Ramsey+, which connects to your bank account, you can speed up the process even further so you never miss a transaction.

When you understand that budgeting aims to give you independence rather than restrict it, you'll be on your way to enjoying your life and your bank account! That is what we mean when we say "winning with money."

## How To Make Budgeting Fun

Many people love budgeting and would not want to live without it anymore (Yes, I confess to being one of them as budgeting served me very well over the years).

However, other people dread budgeting as they are afraid of the extra work, complexities, and presumed restrictions a life with a budget might entail. But it does not have to be this way. Here are some ideas to make it more enjoyable and exciting:

1. **Recall your why**

- Remind yourself why you are using a budget, to begin with.

- Remember the benefits a budget can deliver and your expectations regarding how it is supposed to serve you.
- Specifically, think of your goals and the fact that a budget will bring you much closer to accomplishing them. These types of thoughts should inspire you to continue and make budgeting your very own success story.

### 2. Don't overdo it

Perfection is the enemy of the good. While you might need to be highly detailed in your early days of budgeting, you are better off to work with rounded numbers over time. Don't use decimals. This will kill you. Eventually, you will no longer feel the need to track every single penny. The more your confidence grows, the more flexible budgeting will become.

### 3. Have fun

- Allow for some amusements in your budget. No matter how tight your budget might be, there should always be something reserved to enjoy. It does not have to cost a fortune.
- Make room in your budget to have some fun. This keeps you motivated.

### 4. Limit administration

Do yourself a favor and reduce formalities using technology (a suitable electronic budget spreadsheet or a budget software/app). Without becoming too obsessed with the tool itself, now and then, do enjoy a good (pie) chart or (bar) graph illustrating your earning, spending, and saving behavior. Digitalization is not only appealing, but its practicality also decreases your time involvement and stress levels.

### 5. Introduce budget dates

- Set up a fixed date in your calendar for a regular budget day or night.
- Make this event special, something to look forward to.
- Pick a great location to go through the numbers.

### 6. Find a budget buddy

If you have someone you can genuinely trust (your partner, a family member, a true friend), go through budget dates together. Share experiences and hold each other accountable.

7. **Reward yourself**

Once a goal or any other budget milestone is achieved, treat yourself. Such rewards raise your mood and keep you going. If you have a budget buddy, celebrate together.

8. **Make it a game**

You can turn budgeting into a game and challenge yourself (or one another if you have a budget buddy). For example, you could target to come in below budget for the next month by trying to save 20% more (or spend 20% less) than your current budget. As an incentive, you could allow yourself to spend half of the achieved savings on (additional) entertainment (delivering short-term gratification) while putting the other half in your savings account (delivering long-term benefits).

As you see, budgeting does not have to be boring. There are ways to spice up the exercise. Maybe you have additional ideas on your own that can further motivate you. Be creative but do keep your eyes on the ball, I mean on the budget.

Living with a budget does not have to be dull. Reserve some funds in your budget for entertainment, use technology to reduce bureaucracy, eliminate decimals from your budget, turn budget nights into a special event, search for a budget buddy, reward yourself for achieved milestones, and perform budget challenges as if it were a game.

## Habits To Adopt To Start Saving Money

When choosing it's an ideal opportunity to begin setting aside cash, individuals start looking for changed approaches to get this going. Some beginning was searching for that sorcery ticket that should lead them directly to riches and joy. Others understand it's an extraordinary chance to begin taking out waste, obligation, and pointless things.

While everybody's excursion to "achievement" is somewhat unique, there's one thing that all fruitful individuals share practically speaking, and that is good propensities.

The ideal approach to set up great life propensities is by pausing for a minute and taking a gander at your life. Do you have a cash mentality? Have you set up propensities that will assist your life objectives? To arrive at the spot, you need to be monetary; you must have to fabricate your mentality around how you will come.

### 9. Speak the truth About Your Bad Habits

The central propensity you can learn is to confront reality. You haven't had the option to put something aside for quite a while because you've postponed tolerating current realities. I get it; it is difficult to acknowledge you're not saving however much you ought to. It's simpler to overlook this and go through the cash you could be saving, trusting you'll have sufficient extra.

Feel free to concede to yourself you've been deceiving yourself for quite a while.

This isn't to cause yourself to feel awful. Be pleased with yourself for being straightforward and show self-sympathy. Presently you're mindful you convey negative behavior patterns, and it's an ideal opportunity to work

### 10. Perceive Your Money Mentality

When you hear "investment funds," what rings a bell?

- Do you get energized because you're on target for retirement? Or, on the other hand, do you wince realizing you have been squandering your cash these previous few weeks?
- You're not saving a direct result of the narratives you're playing in your mind. Set some time in your schedule to talk with yourself.
- Sort out what cash stories you've been advising yourself and challenge them. For instance, if you trust, you ought to go through your cash as it comes—ask how this has brought about the most recent couple of years. You will likely provoke awful cash stories to make better ones.

### 11. Characterize Your Needs and Wants

It's alright to like expensive brands. The issue is attempting to purchase everything since you need to stay aware of loved ones. As Paula Pant states, "you can manage the cost of anything other than not all that matters." This is the reason you need to characterize what your requirements and needs are.

Make a rundown of things you need. For instance, PDAs, and food, house needs. At that point, make your rundown of needs for perfect quality shoes, the most recent cell phone, and so on.

It would be best if you were not accepting everything from your needs list right away. All things being equal, pick one and make a spending plan for it. Set aside cash first and award yourself with an item from your "needs" list whenever you've arrived at a reserve funds objective

### 12. Comprehend Your Cash Flow Using Top Tools

You may trust you comprehend your income (cash coming and out of your record.) You get paid two times a month and spend an approximated measure of your compensation on costs. The lay sits on an equal financial balance without reason. This is a catastrophe waiting to happen.

All things being equal, use cash following applications to follow your income better. Sync up the entirety of your records and let Personal Capital wrap up.

### 13. Figure out How to Set SMART objectives

Suppose you need to arrive at your drawn-out monetary objectives. In that case, you initially need to distinguish what they are and afterward think of how much cash you'll have to contact them. Smart economic goals are gainful for this. Intelligent objectives are Specific, Measurable, Attainable, Realistic, and Timely.

It will be much more strenuous to get to where you need to be if you don't make a specific plan and set attainable objectives. With SMART goals, you are making an activity arrangement to get the things done you need. It is safe to say that you know about defining monetary objectives? Consider both your present moment and long-haul needs, and set yourself up with something that works for you.

"I need to be rich" isn't SMART. Nor is "I need to be a mogul." But, "I need to save $500,000 inside the following two years" is SMART.

For instance, have you contemplated setting aside cash in a retirement account or a secret stash? By keeping money in one of these records, you shield yourself from unsafe monetary circumstances later on. Expressing you need to resign upbeat isn't sufficient. You need to set SMART objectives. Consider SMART objectives as ones you can make a move on and track. The reason for making SMART objectives is to have the option to keep tabs on your development. By what other means would you know whether you've arrived at your saving objectives? Survey your present monetary goals and make them SMART.

### 14. Use Tools to Track Your Expenses

If you don't know how to manage your money correctly, you'll most likely waste it. Your objective should be to keep your costs as low as expected while having a top-level salary. The issue is you may not survey your accounts routinely. Along these lines, you may be overpaying for your administrations.

Once more, you can follow costs utilizing cash following application, showing you the sum you go through every month.

### 15. Figure out How to Negotiate Your Bills

When you're following your costs, make it a stride further. Possibilities are you might be overpaying for your administrations or pay for ones you needn't bother with. Arranging your cost isn't hard. I diminished my wireless bill by $10 each month with a 5-minute call.

You can do likewise. Setting aside cash with your bills implies you'll have more money to save. Coordinate your cost from the costliest to the least.

At that point, begin calling your most costly specialist co-ops to arrange your bills. If you forget to organize the first run-through, hang up and try again. A large portion of your specialist organizations will be huge organizations, so you'll work with an alternate individual each time. You additionally have the choice to utilize administrations like Trim, who haggle for your benefit. In any case, don't agree to what you're paying now and arrange your costs.

You can arrange large numbers of your bills. With a touch of examination, inspiration, and some assurance, you can contact the different organizations you work with and negotiate a lower rate.

### 16. Be Frugal with Your Money

It's alright to utilize your cash to purchase things that fulfill you.

However, if you're still not saving enough after cutting your costs, you'll need to try a different approach. I'm against embracing moderation for doing as such.

However, being parsimonious isn't double. There are various levels to moderation. In case you're experiencing difficulty saving, search for zones where you can cut more. For instance, rather than paying for Netflix, observe free recordings on YouTube.

Rehash this cycle until there are no more zones left. Cutting administrations and being thriftier than your acclimated is just brief. When you're ready to save more, you can return to the administrations you love.

**17. Switch over to No Credit Card**

The obligation is regularly the explanation a large portion of us can't save. You may acquire fair pay, yet once you factor in your lease, vehicle note, and Mastercard's, you're left with pretty much nothing. The regular Mastercard obligation is around $16,000. The ideal approach to keep a strategic distance from Mastercard obligation is to quit utilizing it by and large.

Disregard acquiring focuses. Avoid your charge card at home someplace with regards to locate.

### 18. Audit Your Financial Progress Daily

You need to audit your funds every day. With cash following applications, you're ready to do this with no issue. Regardless of whether you don't audit your accounts every day, make a suggestion to check where you stand once each week or month.

To energize this propensity, make surveying your funds fun. For instance, check them while eating your #1 food. Or, on the other hand, reward yourself with something little from your "needs" list. Once checking on your funds turns into a propensity, you'll be in an ideal situation to save more.

### 19. Prepare Your Lunch to Save cash

A $10 feast doesn't appear to be a ton. It might even feel like a deal, contingent upon how great your food was. The issue is doing this 5 times each week, now and then even two times a day. Out of nowhere, your $1o suppers cost you $200+ each month.

Make it a propensity to put together your lunch to work. Pick one day during the week to dinner prep for the whole week and watch your investment funds develop.

### 20. Influence Tools to Cut Junk Mail

In case you're indistinguishable from a great many people, you browse your email a couple of times each day. Organizations go through a bunch of cash to guarantee you think about their most recent deals. This will just make you need to spend more.

To dodge the compulsion to spend, withdraw from the vast majority of these organizations. On the other hand, make a different organizer inside your email supplier that is far away. Use administrations like unroll—me to effectively withdraw from limited-time messages.

### 21. Receive the 3o-Day Rule

Have you at any point bought something just to lament the deal a couple of days after the fact? Assuming this is the case, the 3o-day Rule is for you. Each time you will make another buy put it in a safe spot for 3o days. If following 3o days, you need to purchase this thing, do it. This will not stop every terrible buy, yet it will cut the silliest ones.

### 22. Work on Important Tasks, Not Everything

Time is the solitary asset you have that cash can't accept. This is the reason you need to ensure it no matter what. In case you're straightforward with yourself, you're not gainful with your time. Watching supportive YouTube recordings or investing energy with companions isn't time squandered. The issue is doing just these.

This isn't an issue if you're already financially secure. However, if you want to save more money, you'll need to be more efficient with your time. How do you do it?

Like cash, you need to follow it. Use time following applications to find out about how you're investing your energy. Expect to invest a portion of your energy dealing with your cash better and looking for changed approaches to develop.

### 23. Be a Voracious Reader

You're not setting aside sufficient cash because you don't know about every dollar's latent capacity.

For instance, on the off chance that you'd put $1,000 in the securities exchange, it would twofold inside 10 years. Many don't know this and would instead place their cash in a regular bank account. You don't should be a monetary master; however, you need to comprehend cash essentials.

### 24. Develop an Emergency Fund

Do you realize what will occur sooner or later in your life? An unexpected crisis cost. What's more, when that second comes, the exact opposite thing you'll need to stress over is the way to pay for it.

On the off chance that you're required to advance your monetary circumstance and set yourself up for progress, you need a just-in-case account sufficiently large to pay at any rate 3 months of costs, ideally 6—no exceptional cases. This is this present reality, and it is loaded with things like occupation misfortune, clinical costs, and family crises. Also, by and large, there is no way to forestall them. However, you ought to get ready for them monetarily.

Try not to be the individual saying, "I never figured it would happen to me." Be the individual saying, "Thank heavens I was readied."

It is alright for a crisis to astound you inwardly; however, there is no explanation it should astonish you monetarily. Go set up another currency market record, and begin constructing a just-in-case account.

### 25. Set Financial Goals

If you don't set monetary objectives, what precisely would you say you are running after? Also, how would you anticipate keeping tabs on your development? Getting prone to set monetary objectives is perhaps the main things you can do in an individual budget. What's more, it is one of the primary cash propensities for the well-off.

However, recall, cash isn't a 'ballpark it' sort of game. Defining an objective like "I need to get rich" is certainly not a decent objective. I'm supportive of you getting affluent, yet it's impossible to quantify your prosperity and progress with an aim like that. Set an objective of saving $10 million for retirement before you turn 60. You can work in reverse to decide precisely how much cash you need to contribute each month and the return rate you need to accomplish reliably. At that point, you can keep tabs on your development en-route and cause acclimations to guarantee you to arrive.

Seth Godin said, "... individuals who complete things, who lead, who develop and who have an effect — those individuals have objectives." On the off chance that you're required to lead, develop, and affect your accounting records, start defining objectives.

### 26. Improve Your Money Skills to Grow Your Income

There's a cutoff to how much cash you can save, yet not how much money you can acquire. This is the reason you need to begin a side business. T

he web has made it conceivable to assemble a business as an afterthought while working regular work. Decide to establish a business in an industry you're acquainted with.

Will it be simple? No, yet worth the exertion. In case you're as yet ignorant regarding where to begin, here are some business thoughts.

## 27. Pay More Than the Minimum on Your Credit Cards

Make a propensity from now into the foreseeable future to put nothing on your Mastercard on the off chance that you cannot take care of the whole equilibrium around the same time. Dreadfully numerous individuals wind up in credit obligation due to their awful ways of managing money.

What's more, talking about Visas, if you need to turn out to be monetarily steady, you should dispose of those adjusts. If you have not been fruitful in taking care of your charge cards before, at that point, you ought to focus on paying more than the base installment due.

## 28. Focus on those financial records.

At the lower part of numerous assertions, they will regularly reveal to you what amount of time it will require to take care of your equilibrium on the off chance that you just compensation the base installment and what amount of time it will need on the off chance that you pay a fixed sum somewhat higher than the base installment. More often than not, there's a distinction of quite a long while!

## 29. Figure out how to Say "No" to Yourself

This is a critical one. I nearly rate this one with as much significance as living inside your methods. If you're not ready to advise yourself "no," it will be difficult for you to oversee your funds. Saying no is tied to controlling the driving forces when you are shopping or barely making the rounds.

Making only 20 motivation buys each month at a normal of "just" $5 amounts to $100 spent on stuff you needn't bother with. That is $100, which isn't going into reserve funds or ventures or to settling obligation. One stunt you can utilize is the "72 Hour Rule". If you believe you need to buy something, you must wait 72 hours before making your purchase.

# CHAPTER EIGHT

# How To Smartly Invest Your Saved Money

Once you have saved up some money, the next you should consider is, what are you going to do with those? This chapter dives into various ways of helping you understand what you can do with your leftover money.

## Ideas To Utilize Leftover Money

### 1. Roll the Cash Over

The first choice for surplus budget money is to roll it into the next month's budget. After all, if you were diligent enough to stick within your budget, why not make your life easier by allowing yourself some wiggle room?

For example, you could put the money into your next grocery budget to not have to scrimp on food as much. Alternatively, you might put the money into a miscellaneous budgeting fund to relieve some of the burdens on various budgeting categories.

Rolling over extra budget money into the next month is a fantastic choice that will help to simplify your financial life. Furthermore, suppose you manage to stick to your budget month after month. In that case, your remaining funds will serve as a financial buffer for any unforeseen budgeting mishaps.

### 2. Pay Off Your Debts

Getting out of debt is one of the best financial choices you can make; the sooner you do it, the better.

So, if you have any debt, use your remaining budget money to pay it off as soon as possible. I'm not only referring to credit cards. If you owe money on a car, boat, RV, home, or something else, throw every penny you have at it.

In reality, being able to pay extra against debt should be one of your key reasons for coming in under budget each month.

Getting out of debt is one of the most liberating, relieving, and profitable financial steps you can take. So get to work.

3. **Launch a Side Business**

There are a plethora of side businesses you can get into these days that have low start-up costs. Suppose you want to work as a virtual assistant, a freelancer, a writer, or something else. In that case, your extra budget money will most likely get you there.

For example, if you want to start a WordPress blog, all you really need is a positive attitude and a few dollars per month for hosting. Furthermore, you could use the extra budget money to pay for an online class to improve your blogging skills or even a small amount of marketing.

Starting a side business is a perfect way to use up some extra cash in your budget. Who knows, you could even start a side business that becomes your full-time work one day.

4. **Increase Your Emergency Fund**

Would you have enough savings if you lost your job tomorrow to support yourself (and your family) for the next few months? If not, it might be time to consider setting up an emergency fund.

A solid emergency fund is one of the most important foundations of a healthy financial situation. We recommend that you save enough money to cover your living expenses for the next six months. So, if you have money left over from your spending, putting it in your emergency fund is a smart idea.

It might not be the most enjoyable way to spend the extra cash, but if the time comes when you need it, you will be incredibly grateful.

### 5. Give Yourself a Break

I don't think it's a secret that budgeting can be tedious at times. I'd be lying if I said it didn't. And the tighter your budget, the stale your life will get. However, there is a solution, and it is known as fun money.

Every budget should include a category for the money you get to spend on recreation or items that bring you joy. And suppose you are highly diligent during the month and have some money left over. In that case, it is perfectly acceptable to spend it on something nice.

My wife, for example, enjoys shopping for shoes and clothing, while I enjoy shopping for woodworking equipment. We really enjoy going out on a fancy date every now and then. So, if we ever have a budgeting surplus, you could find us spending it on one of those things.

There is no harm in rewarding yourself. On the opposite, it can be a powerful motivator to stick to a budget.

### 6. Put Money Away For A Car

I can almost guarantee that you will need or want a new car at some stage in your life. (When I say new, I mean 'new to you.') Furthermore, any car eventually requires new tires, repairs, or simply a routine maintenance, which is why using leftover budget money for car expenses is a great choice.

### 7. Put It to Work

Investing is one of the best things you can do with your extra budget money if you are debt-free (except for your mortgage). Why is this so? Since even a small amount of money left to earn interest over time will grow to impressive proportions.

For example, if you were to spend an additional $50 every month for the next 30 years and earn a 10% annual return, your money will rise to more than $100,000. That's not bad, given we're just talking about your extra cash.

If you decide to invest your capital, here are three excellent options:

- Retiring
- College Savings Plan
- Index ETFs

a) **Retiring**

This is perhaps the most obvious and easiest way to spend your budget surplus. Suppose you have a 401(k), IRA, or another type of retirement account. In that case, even a small amount of extra money will make a significant difference.

b) **College Savings Plan**

Try putting the extra budget money into a 529 plan if you have children and want to help them pay for college. It is a tax-advantaged savings account that allows the money to grow tax-free as long as it is used to pay for college.

### c) Index ETFs

Index funds are a great place to start if you are uncertain or nervous about investing. They are basically mutual funds designed to replicate a certain index (i.e., the S&P 500). Index funds also come with the added bonus of low expense ratios, appealing to any investor.

## 8. Make a Vacation Plan

Travel is also one of the most powerful motivators for people to start living on a budget. There is so much to see in this world. Plus, there's something special about getting away from it all for a week or two every year to recharge your battery. However, if you want to travel extensively, you will need funds.

That is why you should consider placing some money left over from your budget into a travel fund.

**Consider this**: if you can squeeze an additional $100 out of your budget each month, you'll save $1,200 a year. Add that to the money you're already putting aside for a travel fund, and you've got yourself a pretty fantastic annual break.

### 9. Give a Little More

I believe we should all agree that the pursuit of money can be a hazardous game. It has the potential to distort people's minds and become the focal point of their whole lives. Unfortunately, I believe this is the standard rather than the exception. Cash, on the other hand, can be used for some truly amazing stuff. Money is merely a weapon. What matters is what you want to do about it.

I truly believe that generosity contributes significantly to financial contentment and, eventually, financial prosperity. Giving is vital for your financial life, spiritual life, and relationships, whether you give to your local church or donate money to a worthy cause.

While giving should be the first thing you do with any money you earn, you can also use any leftover budget money to give a little more.

### 10. Contribute to Your Gift and Party Fund

Throughout the year, you will most likely take part in a number of holidays, birthdays, and spontaneous celebrations. Which each comes with its own collection of costs. So, if you do have extra money in your budget, consider putting it into a gift and party fund.

Can you imagine going into the Christmas season with enough money to purchase all of your presents ahead of time?

How convenient would it be to simply withdraw funds from a party fund any time you needed to purchase a bottle of wine for a dinner party?

It's a good little bonus if you can use your extra money to pay for these kinds of expenses.

## Smart Investment Ideas For Short Term

Suppose you're looking to invest money in the short term. In that case, you're probably looking for a secure location to stash cash before you need it in the not-too-distant future. The volatile markets and slumping economy in 2020 drove many investors to hold cash as the coronavirus crisis raged on and 2021 could be a rocky year as the economy tries to regain lost ground.

As a result, instead of squandering the money on a potentially risky investment, you'll want to make sure you have it when you need it. So, in a short-term investment, the most important thing investors should look for is safety.

When you make a short-term investment, you always do so because you need the money at a specific moment. If you're saving for a down payment on a house or a wedding, for example, you must have the funds available. Short-term investments are those made for fewer than three years. You'll forego a potentially higher return in exchange for the security of getting the capital.

Suppose you have a longer period – at least three to five years (and longer is preferable). In that case, you might consider investing in stocks. Stocks have the potential for significantly higher returns. For long periods, the stock market rises by an average of 10% every year – but it is more unpredictable. As a result, the longer period allows you to ride out the stock market's ups and downs.

However, safety comes at a cost. You are unable to benefit as much from a short-term investment as you will from a long-term investment. If you invest in the short term, you would be restricted to those forms of investments and avoid riskier investments such as stocks and stock funds. (However, if you're willing to invest for the long term, here's how to buy stocks.)

However, there are a few benefits of making short-term investments. They are frequently highly liquid, allowing you to get your money anytime you need it. They are also less risky than long-term investments, so you might have little to no downside.

1. **Open Up An Savings Account**

A savings account at a bank or credit union is a better option than keeping cash in a checking account, which usually offers very little interest on deposits. A savings account can earn interest regularly from the bank.

Savings accounts should be compared, so it is simple to find which banks offer the highest interest rates and open one.

Risk: Savings accounts are FDIC-insured at banks and NCUA-insured at credit unions, so you will not lose money. These accounts pose no immediate danger, but investors who hold their money for longer periods will struggle to keep up with inflation.

Savings accounts are extremely liquid, and you can add money to them at any time. On the other hand, Savings accounts normally allow for a maximum of six fee-free withdrawals or transfers per statement period. (As part of its emergency market interventions, the Federal Reserve has permitted banks to waive this requirement.) Of course, you'll want to keep an eye out for banks that charge fees for managing the account or using ATMs so that you can avoid them.

2. **Invest In Short-Term Corporate Bond Funds**

Corporate bonds are debt securities issued by large companies to finance their investments. They are usually regarded as healthy and pay interest regularly, such as quarterly or twice a year.

Bond funds are portfolios of corporate bonds from various corporations, usually from various industries and sizes. Because of this diversification, a poor performing bond would not significantly impact the total return. The bond fund would payout interest consistently.

Risk: Since a short-term corporate bond fund is not government-insured, it may lose money. On the other hand, bonds are relatively secure, particularly if you buy a diverse portfolio. Furthermore, a short-term fund has the least amount of risk exposure to changing interest rates, so rising or declining rates would not significantly impact the fund's price.

Short-term corporate bond funds are extremely liquid, and they can be purchased and sold every day the stock market is open.

### 3. Explore Money Market Accounts

Money market accounts are a form of bank deposit that normally pays a higher interest rate than savings accounts, but they often have a higher minimum investment requirement.

Risk: Look for an FDIC-insured money market account so that your funds are safe from loss, with coverage of up to $250,000 per depositor, per bank.

The main risk for money market funds, including savings accounts, happens over time because their low-interest rates make it difficult for investors to keep up with inflation. However, in the short term, this is not a major concern.

Money market accounts are extremely liquid, though federal regulations still place certain withdrawal limits.

4. **Explore Cash Management Accounts**

A cash management account, similar to an omnibus account, allows you to invest in a range of short-term investments. You can frequently invest, write checks from the account, transfer money, and perform other typical banking functions. Robo-advisors and online stock brokers are popular providers of cash management accounts.

As a result, the cash management account provides you with a great deal of versatility.

Danger: Since cash management accounts are often invested in secure low-yield money market funds, there is little risk. Some robo-advisor accounts deposit your money into FDIC-protected partner banks, so make sure you don't exceed FDIC deposit coverage if you already do business with one of the partner banks.

Cash management accounts are highly liquid, allowing money to be withdrawn at any moment. In this regard, they can outperform conventional savings and money market accounts, which have monthly withdrawal limits.

5. **Explore Short Term, U.S Government Bonds**

Government bonds are similar to corporate bonds except that they are issued by the federal government of the United States and its agencies. Government bond funds buy investments from government-sponsored companies such as Fannie Mae and Freddie Mac, such as T-bills, T-bonds, T-notes, and mortgage-backed securities. These bonds are regarded as low-risk.

Risk: Although these bonds are not FDIC-insured, they are the government's commitments to repay the money. These bonds are considered very secure since they are backed by the full faith and credit of the United States.

Furthermore, by investing in a short-term bond fund, an investor assumes a low level of interest rate risk. As a result, rising or dropping interest rates would have little effect on the price of the fund's bonds.

Government bond funds are highly liquid since government bonds are among the most commonly traded assets on exchanges. They are available for purchase and sale every day that the stock market is open.

### 6. Invest In Certificates Of Deposit

Certificates of deposit, or CDs, are available at your bank and typically provide a higher rate of return than other bank products such as savings accounts and money market accounts.

CDs are time deposits, which means that when you open one, you agree to keep the money in the account for a set period, ranging from a few weeks to several years, depending on the maturity you choose. The bank will pay you a higher interest rate in return for the convenience of keeping this money in its vault.

The bank pays interest on the CD regularly, and at the end of the contract, the bank returns the principal plus interest gained.

**Risk:** CDs are FDIC-insured, so you would not lose any money if you buy them. The risks of a short-term CD are small, but one risk is that you can lose out on a better rate elsewhere while your money is locked up in the CD. If the interest rate is too low, you will lose buying power due to inflation.

CDs are less liquid than the other bank investments on this list. When you agree to the terms of the CD, you usually grant the bank the right to charge you a penalty for terminating the CD early.

But you should be extra cautious not to tie up your money and then find yourself having to access it before the term is up.

### 7. Invest In Treasurys

Treasurys are available in three varieties: T-bills, T-bonds, and T-notes, and they provide the ultimate in secure yield, backed by the federal government's AAA credit rating. Depending on your needs, you might choose to buy individual securities rather than a government bond fund.

Individual bonds, like bond funds, are not insured by the FDIC but are backed by the government's pledge to repay the capital, making them rather secure.

Liquidity: US government bonds are the most liquid bonds on the market, and they can be traded every day the market is open.

## What Should A Good Short-Term Investment Have

Good short-term investments can share several characteristics, but they are usually distinguished by the three following characteristics:

- **Stability:** Good short-term investments do not fluctuate excessively or are extremely volatile, as many stocks and bonds are. The money will be there when you need it, and it is also insured by the FDIC or guaranteed by the government.

- **Liquidity**: A successful short-term investment would typically have high liquidity, which means you will be able to access the cash invested in it quickly. In the case of such investments, such as CDs, you will be notified when the money becomes available, and you may still redeem the CD, but there could be a tax.
- **Low transaction costs:** Unlike a home, a successful short-term investment does not cost a lot of money to move into or out of. This is particularly significant given the historically low yields on short-term investments.

These characteristics imply that your capital will not be at risk and will be available when you need it, one of the primary reasons for making a short-term investment.

On the other hand, long-term investments will yield a higher return but must withstand greater short-term volatility. If you really need the money, you can have to sell at a loss to get it.

# Smart Investment Ideas For The Long Term

Investing is one of the best ways to protect the financial future, and one of the best ways to invest is over time. With the ups and downs of 2020, it might be tempting to take a break in 2021. However, the economy is still recovering, and it is more important than ever to concentrate on long-term investing and stick to your game plan.

Although many people think of investing as attempting to make a quick buck in the stock market, it is through long-term investing that everyday investors can really create wealth. You will achieve your financial goals and improve your financial stability by looking and saving long term.

Today's investors have several options for investing their money and can select the amount of risk they are willing to take to meet their needs. You can choose between very secure options like a certificate of deposit (CD) and increasing the risk – and possible return! – with investments like stocks and equity mutual funds or ETFs.

Or you can do a little bit of both, diversifying your portfolio so that it performs well in almost every investment climate.

Although long-term investment can lead to a stable future, you must consider the value of risk and time horizon to achieve your financial goals.

To earn a higher return on investment, you must usually take on more risk. As a result, very safe investments like CDs tend to have low yields, while medium-risk assets like bonds have slightly higher yields, and high-risk stocks have higher returns. Investors seeking a higher return would typically need to take on more risk.

Although stocks as a whole have a solid track record – the Swamp; P 500 index has returned 10% over long periods – stocks are well-known for their volatility. It is not uncommon for a stock to fluctuate by 50 percent in a single year, either up or down. (Some of the safest short-term investments are much less risky.)

Can you tolerate a higher degree of risk in exchange for a higher return? It is important to understand your risk tolerance and panic if your assets fall in value. If an investment has the potential to grow, you should avoid selling it while it is down. It can be disheartening to sell an investment just to see it grow even further.

One way to reduce your risk is to commit to keeping your assets for a longer period. The longer holding period allows you to ride out the market's ups and downs. While the index has a strong track record, those returns came over time, and the index could be down significantly in a short period. As a result, investors who bring money into the market should be able to keep it there for at least three to five years, preferably longer.

As a result, you can use time as a powerful ally in your investing. You don't have to spend any of your time monitoring your investments and worrying about short-term movements, which is also beneficial for those who commit to investing for the long term. You can build a long-term strategy and then (mostly) place it on autopilot.

### 1. Investing In Growth Stocks

Growth stocks are the Ferraris of the stock investment universe. They pledge rapid growth as well as high investment returns. Growth stocks are frequently technology firms, although they do not have to be. They usually reinvest all of their earnings, so they rarely pay out dividends, at least not until their growth slows.

Growth stocks can be risky since investors often pay a high price for the stock about the company's earnings. As a result, when a bear market or a recession occurs, these stocks will lose a significant amount of value very rapidly. It's as if their sudden fame vanished in a heartbeat. Growth stocks, on the other hand, have historically been among the strongest performers.

If you're going to buy individual growth stocks, you'll need to do a thorough business analysis, which can take a long time. And, since growth stocks are volatile, you'll need to have a high-risk tolerance or commit to keeping the stocks for at least three to five years.

Risk/reward: Since investors are willing to pay a high price for growth stocks, they are among the riskier segments of the market. As a result, when the going gets rough, these stocks have a tendency to plunge. However, the world's largest businesses – the Facebooks, Alphabets, and Amazons – have all become high-growth companies, so the future reward is endless if you can find the right business.

2. **Investing In Stock Funds**

If you don't want to spend the time and money researching individual stocks, a stock fund – either an ETF or a mutual fund – may be a good alternative. When you invest in a widely diversified fund, such as an index fund or a Nasdaq-100 index fund, you will receive many high-growth stocks as well as many others. However, you would have a more diverse and safe portfolio than if you only owned a few individual stocks.

A mutual fund is an ideal option for an investor who wishes to be more involved but does not have the time or desire to devote to investing full-time. Furthermore, when purchasing a stock portfolio, you will receive the weighted average return of all the companies in the fund, so the fund will be less volatile than if you had just owned a few stocks.

If you purchase a not widely diversified fund – for example, a fund focused on a single sector – you should be mindful that your fund would be less diversified than one based on a large index such as the S&P 500. As a result, if you bought a fund focusing on the automobile industry, it could have a high level of exposure to oil prices. If oil prices increase, many of the stocks in the fund may suffer.

Risk/reward: Investing in a mutual fund is less expensive than purchasing individual stocks, and it often requires less effort. However, it can still jump quite a bit in any given year, perhaps losing as much as 30% or even gaining 30% in some of its more severe years.

To be sure, a mutual fund is less work to own and manage than individual stocks, but since you own more companies – and not all of them can succeed in any given year – the returns should be more consistent. A mutual fund would also provide you with a lot of future upsides. The following are some of the best index funds.

### 3. Investing In Bond Funds

A bond fund, such as a mutual fund or an exchange-traded fund (ETF), holds a wide range of bonds from various issuers. Bond funds are usually classified based on the type of bond in the fund – the size, riskiness, issuer (corporate, municipality, or federal government), and other factors. So, if you're looking for a bond fund, you have several options to choose from.

When a corporation or government issues a bond, it promises to pay a fixed interest rate to the bond's owner annually. After the bond's life, the lender repays the bond's principal, and the bond is repaid.

Bonds are one of the safest assets, and bonds become much safer when they are part of a portfolio. Since a fund can own hundreds of different bond types from many different issuers, it diversifies its holdings and lessens the effect of any one bond defaulting on the portfolio.

Although bonds can fluctuate, a bond fund would be relatively stable, though it will shift in response to changes in the prevailing interest rate. Bonds are thought to be safer than bonds, but not all issuers are the same. Government issuers, particularly the federal government, are regarded as relatively stable, while the riskiness of corporate issuers may vary from slightly less to significantly riskier.

The return on a bond or bond fund is usually much lower than the return on a stock fund, maybe 4 to 5 percent per year on government bonds, but less on corporate bonds. It's also much less dangerous.

### 4. Investing In Dividend Stocks

Whereas growth stocks are the sports cars of the stock market, dividend stocks are the sedans – they can deliver decent returns but are unlikely to accelerate as quickly as growth stocks.

A dividend stock is simply one that pays a dividend — a monthly cash payout — regularly. Many stocks pay dividends, but they are more common in larger, more stable firms with less need for capital. Dividend stocks are common with older investors because they provide a consistent income, and the best stocks increase their dividends over time, allowing you to gain more than you would with a bond's fixed payout. REITs are a common form of dividend stock.

Risk/reward: While dividend stocks are less volatile than growth stocks, don't assume they won't fluctuate dramatically, particularly if the stock market enters a rough patch. On the other hand, a dividend-paying stock is typically more mature and developed than a growth company and is generally regarded as safer. However, suppose a dividend-paying company does not earn enough to cover its dividend. In that case, it will reduce the payout, and its stock price will fall as a result.

The payout is the main attraction of a dividend stock, and some of the best businesses pay 2 or 3 percent annually, sometimes more. But, most importantly, they will increase their payouts by 8 or 10% every year for long periods, meaning you'll get a raise every year. The returns here can be high, but not as high as in growth stocks. If you want to buy a diversified range of stocks, there are plenty of dividend stock funds to choose from.

### 5. Investing In Target-Date Funds

If you don't want to handle your own portfolio, target-date funds are a great choice. As you get older, these funds become more conservative, making your portfolio safer as you get closer to retirement when you need the money. When your target date approaches, these funds gradually move your assets from more bullish stocks to more cautious bonds.

Target-date funds are a common option in many workplace 401(k) programs, but they can also be purchased outside of those plans. You choose your retirement year, and the fund takes care of the rest.

Risk/reward: Since target-date funds are essentially a blend of stock and bond funds, they would have many of the same risks. If your goal date is decades out, your fund will hold a higher proportion of stocks, making it more volatile at first. When the target date approaches, the fund will turn toward bonds, causing it to fluctuate less but benefit less.

Since a target-date fund increasingly shifts toward more bonds over time, it is likely to begin underperforming the stock market by a growing margin. You're preceding return in exchange for protection. And, since bonds yield less and less these days, you are more likely to outlive your assets.

To prevent this possibility, some financial advisors suggest investing in a target-date fund that is five or ten years after the date you plan to retire so that you can benefit from the extra growth from stocks.

### 6. Investing In Real Estate

Real estate is the prototypical long-term investment in several respects. It costs a lot of money to get started, the commissions are very substantial, and the returns are only obtained by keeping an asset for a long time rather than a few years. Nonetheless, according to one Bankrate report, real estate was Americans' favorite long-term investment in 2019.

Real estate can be an appealing property, in part because you can borrow money from the bank and pay it back over time. This is particularly common now that interest rates are near historic lows. For those who choose to be their own boss, owning a property allows them to do so, and several tax laws favor property owners in particular.

However, while real estate is often thought of as a passive investment, if you plan on renting out the land, you may need to do a lot of active management.

Risk/reward: When you borrow large sums of money, you place more pressure on investment to perform well. Even if you purchase real estate with all cash, you will have a lot of money locked up in one asset, which can cause problems if anything happens to the asset. And suppose you don't have a tenant. In that case, you'll have to continue paying the mortgage and other maintenance expenses out of your own pocket.

Although the risks can be high, the rewards can also be high. Suppose you choose a good property and handle it well. In that case, you will gain several times your investment if you can keep the asset for an extended period. Furthermore, suppose you pay off a property's mortgage. In that case, you will enjoy greater security and cash flow, making the rental property an appealing choice for older buyers. (Here are ten rental property buying tips.)

7. **Investing In Small-Cap Stocks**

Investors are interested in small-cap stocks or stocks of relatively small companies since they can expand rapidly or capitalize on an emerging market over time. In reality, retailing behemoth Amazon started as a small-cap stock and rewarded investors who kept on to the stock handsomely. Small-cap stocks are frequently, but not always, high-growth stocks.

Small-cap stocks, including high-growth stocks, are riskier. Small businesses are riskier because they have less financial resources, less access to capital markets, and less market strength (less brand recognition, for example). However, well-run businesses can do very well for investors, particularly if they can continue to expand and gain size.

Like growth stock investors, investors will always pay a premium for a small-cap stock's earnings, particularly if it has the potential to expand or become a leading business someday. And since a business is so expensive, small-cap stocks can fall precipitously during a market downturn.

If you're going to buy individual firms, you'll need to evaluate them, which takes time and effort. Buying small businesses is not for everybody.

Risk/reward: Small-cap firms can be very unpredictable, with significant fluctuations from year to year. Aside from market fluctuations, the organization is typically less established than a larger company and has fewer financial resources. As a result, small-cap firms are thought to be riskier than medium- and large-cap companies.

## 8. Investing In Robo-Advisor Portfolio

If you don't want to invest yourself and would rather leave it to an experienced specialist, robo-advisors are a great option. In a robo-advisor, you simply deposit money into the robo account, and it invests it for you based on your objectives, period, and risk tolerance. When you first start, you'll fill out some questionnaires, so the robo-advisor knows what you need from the service, and it will then handle the entire operation. The robo-advisor can choose funds, usually low-cost ETFs, and create a portfolio for you.

How much does the service cost you? The robo-management advisor's fee is usually about 0.25 percent a year, plus the expense of any funds in the portfolio. Investment funds charge based on the amount invested, but funds in robo accounts usually charge between 0.06 percent and 0.15 percent, or $6 to $15 per $10,000 invested.

With a robo-advisor, you can configure the account to be as aggressive or conservative as you want. You should go the path if you want all stocks all of the time. If you prefer that the account be solely in cash or a simple savings account, two of the leading robo-advisors – Wealth front and Betterment – also provide that option.

A robo-advisor, on the other hand, will build a widely diversified investment portfolio that can meet your long-term needs.

**Risk/reward:** The risks of a robo-advisor are heavily dependent on your investments. Suppose you invest in a lot of mutual funds, and you have a high-risk tolerance. In that case, you should expect more volatility than if you invest in bonds or cash in a savings account. As a result, the danger is in what you own.

The potential reward on a Robo-advisor account often varies depending on the investments, and it can range from very high if you own only equity funds to very low if you keep safer assets like cash in a savings account. A Robo-advisor will often create a diversified portfolio to provide a more consistent sequence of annual returns, albeit at the expense of a slightly lower total return. (Right now, these are the perfect robo-advisers.)

9. **Investing In IRA CD**

If you are risk-averse and want a guaranteed income with no risk of failure, an IRA CD is a reasonable choice. This investment is simply a CD within an IRA, as the name implies. And, as long as you follow the laws of a tax-advantaged IRA, you'll stop paying taxes on the interest you earn.

Even if your IRA does not include a CD, it is still a wise investment option.

**Danger/reward:** The risk on an IRA CD could not be where you want it to be. When the CD matures, you have virtually no chance of not getting the payout and principal. It's about as risk-free an investment as there is, and the FDIC will guarantee your account at any individual insured institution up to $250,000 per depositor.

The real risk with an IRA CD is not earning enough to keep up with inflation. It's one of the reasons why, if you already have a core CD portfolio, a great strategy actually adds some risk to get a much better long-term return, particularly if you have a long time before you need the money.

## What Makes A Good Long-Term Investment

It's almost always a safe time to invest in the stock market if you keep a long-term outlook and properly diversify your portfolio. This is because the market continues to rise over time, and as the old adage goes, time in the market is more critical than timing the market.

Over the long term, the market (as calculated by the S&P 500 index) has grown at a rate of about 10% per year. The longer you spend, the more likely you are to receive a portion of the return.

But that doesn't mean you can throw all of your money into the market right now. In the short term, it could go dramatically up or down. Instead, it is more sensible to spend regularly, such as once a week or once a month, and to keep adding money over time. You'll use the dollar-cost averaging technique to help ensure that you don't pay too much for anything.

If you invest in your employer-sponsored 401(k) account regularly, you're still using this technique, adding money with each paycheck. The level of consistency and investing discipline is essential for long-term investing.

While investing for the long term can be beneficial at any time, it can be particularly beneficial when stocks have already dropped significantly, such as during recessions. Lower stock prices provide an incentive to purchase stocks at a discount, eventually resulting in higher long-term returns. However, when stocks fall significantly, many investors become too scared to purchase and benefit.

Another reason it's advantageous to invest consistently through thick and thin is that you'll be able to continue adding to your investment even though the price is down, allowing you to possibly score a bargain. However, you must prepare ahead of time to have your brokerage account open and supported.

Long-term investments provide you with the ability to gain more than short-term investments. The catch is that you must maintain a long-term outlook and not be scared out of the market because your investment has declined or you want to sell for a fast profit.

And by concentrating on the long term – promising not to sell your assets when the market falls – you will be able to escape the short-term noise that causes many investors to lose their way. Investors in the S&P 500, for example, who kept on after the massive decline in early 2020 may have broken even, and then some, in less than a year. You will ride out the hiccups by concentrating on the long term.

Investing for the long term also means that you don't have to keep your eyes on the market all the time, as short-term traders do. You can invest your money on autopilot and then spend your time doing stuff you really enjoy rather than thinking about market movements.

# Please Leave a Review!

I would be incredibly thankful, if you could take just 60 seconds to write a brief review on Amazon. Even it's just a few Sentence!

# CONCLUSION

No matter how much we try and no matter how smartly we keep saving our money, the unfortunate truth is that there will be complications, and there will be various unexpected emergencies that will seem to derail us from our path. I mean, whoever expected COVID to hit us this badly, right?

Regardless of everything, though, the idea is to always have a clear set of goals in mind and bounce back every time an unexpected situation seems to hit.

Suppose, you plan your budget accordingly, though, no matter what type of emergency you face. In that case, you will be able to face it with confidence.

Budgeting is a method of planning how you will spend your earnings. When preparing for your financial goals, budgeting is described as spending less than you earn. Budgeting is the first step toward financial literacy, and thereby financial security and freedom. Budgeting is creating a strategy to invest and save money wisely to achieve your personal and financial goals in life. It should not be viewed as a quantitative exercise that we must endure; rather, it should result from self-evaluation of our relationship with money and a good road map to guide us toward a higher standard and quality of life.

It is the process of matching your expenses and revenue now and for the rest of your life. This budgeting module delves into the nuts and bolts of how someone can learn to make ends meet and plan for a debt-free, financially stable life full of financial stability and independence.

One thing to keep in mind is that a budget is never set in stone. It must be updated regularly to account for new costs that you did not have previously. Perhaps you had any expenses in the last few years that are no longer present in your life. When I first started this budget, I had monthly expenditures, including daycare and diapers, among other things. Now that my children are getting ready to leave for university, I don't have to budget for daycare and diapers. I normally sit down at the beginning of January and prepare for all of the yearly expenditures that I can anticipate we will incur, and then I go from there. Every year, I revise my budget.

It is important to keep track of your budget regularly. It can easily accomplish this with your phone in a matter of minutes. Take a break from social media to ensure that your finances are in order. If you bought fuel for your car, pay it right away with money from all of your different accounts. It works best for me if one of the two people controls the budget and makes sure it stays on track. Cooperation from the other individual is extremely beneficial.

Suppose there is one idea to take away from the concepts discussed in this book. In that case, it is undoubtedly the concept of preparing for your annual expenses during the year. If you simply incorporate this idea into your budget, it can make a significant difference in your life. It's difficult to budget when you have many different yearly expenses that suddenly drop off on your laps.

A balanced budget is a function of priorities, what is important to you as a family. Sure, we'd all like to go on holiday every year or have nice cars, and so on. However, the truth is that you must make difficult decisions on what you can and cannot afford.

"Contante toi avec peu et to seras heureux,"

A good friend of mine who speaks French once told me. This translates to "be comfortable with very little, and you will be happy."

I hope this book has been helpful to you along the way and that you are having more success with your family budget. Money can be a major source of conflict in a relationship. Having a good budget that works would undoubtedly help prevent those long nights sleeping on the couch.

Whether you are struggling financially or looking to ensure a safe future, please, never lose hope! Engrave the concepts provided in this bock in your heart and start implementing them in your life; I promise you that down the line, they will definitely serve you well and give you the financial freedom that you desire.

As a final request, I would encourage you to leave feedback for my book on Amazon if you found this book helpful and effective. It would mean a lot to me and inspire me to produce more high-quality content for you in the future!

**Stay Safe and Stay Blessed.**

# Just For You!

**A FREE GIFT TO OUR READERS**

Ready-to-use templates that you can download and start mind mapping with right away!

**Visit this Link**

https://infobusiness001us.activehosted.com/f/1

Made in the USA
Monee, IL
08 November 2026

67969859R00163